# mystic medusa's
# soul
# mating

Mystic Medusa is an astrologer with a particular interest in the surreal side of star gazing. Her astro guides appear internationally in newspapers, magazines and on the Internet. Her Sun sign is confidential but she does admit to being born in the Chinese Year of the Snake.

Published by Murdoch Books®, a division of Murdoch Magazines Pty Ltd.
©Text Abnorm pty Ltd 2003. ©Design and illustrations Murdoch Books® 2003. All rights reserved.
First published 2003. The author asserts the moral right to be identified as the author of the work.
Mystic Medusa® is a registered trademark of Abnorm pty Ltd.

Chief Executive: Juliet Rogers
Publisher: Kay Scarlett

Creative Director and Design Concept: Marylouise Brammer
Designer: Tracy Laughlin
Illustrations: Tracy Laughlin
Editorial Director: Diana Hill
Editor: Carla Holt
Production Manager: Megan Alsop

National Library of Australia Cataloguing-in-Publication Data
mystic medusa's soulmating
the astro guide to making true love your destiny

ISBN 1 74045 265 8
1. Soul mates. 2. Love. 3. Astrology. I. Mystic Medusa. Astro guide. 133.5

PRINTED IN CHINA by Midas Printing (Asia) Ltd.

Murdoch Books Australia®
GPO Box 1203, Sydney, NSW 2001
Phone: 61 (02) 4352 7000
Fax: 61 (02) 4352 7026

Murdoch Books UK Ltd
Erico House, 6th Floor North,
93-99 Upper Richmond Road,
Putney, London SW15 2TG
Phone: +44 (0) 20 8355 1480
Fax: + 44 (0) 20 8355 1499

DISCLAIMER: The author and the publisher of this work intend the contents of the work to be used for entertainment purposes only and the work must not be used as a professional or counselling resource.

# mystic medusa's

# soul

The astro guide to making true love your destiny

# mating

MURDOCH
**B O O K S**

# Contents

# For 'Us'

'The minute I heard my first love story
I started looking for you not knowing
how blind that was.

Lovers don't finally meet somewhere.
They're in each other all along.'

*The Minute I Heard My First Love Story* – Rumi

# For your eyes only!
# Top-secret astro info

Whether solo or duo, blissfully bonded or longing for love, we are all interested in the concept of soulmating. Do you ever feel as though you just know that your soulmate is out there and wonder what nature of person he or she could be? If in a relationship, do you wonder if your lover is truly The One? Or just the seat-warmer? Wishful thinking wise, wouldn't you love to know how the object of your adoration really feels about you?

This book offers all the inside info about love, romance and, of course, finding your soulmate. Armed with just the date of his or her birth, you can quickly and easily find a person's ideal lover — maybe before even they figure it out — and their soul secrets!

This info is far above and beyond the usual Sun sign compatibility guff. Hello? Don't we all know supposedly so-incompatible Sun signs that are as happy as hell?

Think he's hot? Look him up here. Or have fun figuring out your own subliminal love motivations. Eeek?

Got any friends whose love life defies belief? They could probably do with a spot of soulmating analysis as well! Celeb relationships? Are Reese and Ryan soulmates? You and Ryan? What does Colin Farrell really want in a woman? Is your so-secret love persona the same as Uma's? Or are you more like Nicole?

Confused by Mr There But Not There? Sneak a look at his ideal woman, as determined by the cosmos for the real facts. So in love? Check out the astro-soulmating potential of your liaison! You can do it all through this book!

This secret astro love biz is so simple to learn. Anyone can do it. And you'll be wowed by how freakily accurate it is!

Have fun and blessed be.

Mystic Medusa xxx

# Love in a logical climate

'Launcelot loved Guenevere
from the moment he first beheld her.'

*King Arthur and the Knights of the Round Table* – Doris Ashley

# Love in a logical climate

Physicist Albert Einstein once said that gravitation is not responsible for people falling in love. Love may not make the world go around but it sure feels like it sometimes. Yes, even an official genius like him could grasp that love ain't logical.

Yet the emergence of psychology as a science has also made us suspicious of love. Maybe we feel those first pangs of love and think, 'Eeek, is this some sort of dysfunctional complex?' Somehow, this narcissistic object choice has set off an infantile need for ongoing company ... theirs only! Or maybe the dizzy sensation signifies a wheat allergy? That's it, for sure. It's all to do with insulin levels. No more grains, rice or pasta. No sugar.

Then again, that woozy feeling could be some sort of endocrine disorder. What else but hormones going crazy causes sudden lust attacks in the middle of a workday? Or perhaps an osteopath may be able to fix you up.

Sudden blissful experiences alternating with nervousness? There's medication for that, isn't there?

Shrinks talk of love in terms of codependency, conflict management, long-term relationship, boundaries, working at it, foreplay, bonding ... making love sounds as though it's some sort of hideous day-job gig! Then there is the socio-biology mob who say love at first sight has to do with our pheromones and the

# Soulmating

hip-to-waist ratio of females. Just as apes are drawn to one another by the baring of bottoms, revelation of mammary glands and a show of strength, humans enact complex but essentially banal mating rituals.

Romance, apparently, is just a ploy to ensure population growth. We have no real affinity with a partner and instant attraction is hardwired into our genes – it's simply a tribal impulse. So we're tricked into breeding and then have to somehow forge a productive social unit with our partner.

Another modern love theory is the idea that attachment to another lowers one's higher mind. Romance is simply a low-rent yearning that stops us merging with the Cosmos. Better by far to stay pure through yoga, meditation and celibacy.

Finally, there is the cynical 'romance as sport' belief system. Love is a competition and the best prepped – that is, the most toned, educated, rich, good at sex, etc – scores the best catch. Until, that is, a better contender comes along to challenge our position and take our 'trophy'.

However, most of us have too much poetry in our hearts to subscribe to the above clinical schools of thought. Love is not a dysfunction, a competition, the privilege of mammals or a distraction from our high-falutin' spiritual goals.

Love is all about feelings and emotions. It's the hook that keeps us interested, that adds meaning to the most naff of pop songs and lifts us above the usual round of health warnings, cosmetic colour trends, mismatched socks, geopolitics, cellulite, past use-by dates and letters from the council...

And romance is still the pivotal point around which our personal worlds revolve. The sudden 'zing' of connection with another, that swooning sensation and so scary, 'Wow, I'm in love' realization that is essential to human wellbeing.

True romance turns life back into a fairytale for grown-ups. Falling in love not only feels magical, it elevates our entire being.

The euphoric ideal of happy ever after sustains us through the peaks and (yes!) lows of everyday loving.

It's why even the most jaded and louche among us secretly cherish the concept of having a soulmate.

So, what's it all about, this thing called love? And what exactly is a soulmate?

'Whoever loved that loved not at first sight?'

*Hero and Leander* – Christopher Marlowe

# Soulmating
## 101

'As soon as I met David, I thought, "I want to marry this person, grow up with this person, learn things about life with this person and have a family." I surprised myself.'

Former Spice Girl Victoria Beckham on her husband, soccer star David Beckham

# Soulmating 101

Surprisingly, not every dictionary acknowledges the word soulmate. The ones that do tend toward the dry definition of he or she being a person of 'shared temperament.'

So let's delve deeper and look to history for a more meaningful explanation. Plato's theory of soulmating is probably the best known definition. The ancient Greek soldier-scholar postulated the idea of one soul being made up of a male and female. Split apart, we wander the world, seeking our 'other half' so we may be whole again. This twin-soul motif has recurred in all sorts of belief systems and myths over the centuries.

In the 20th century, Edgar Cayce, one of the world's most famous clairvoyants, popularized the concept behind the 'haven't we met before?' sensation of deja vu. Edgar felt that strong attractions to another were linked to subconscious memory patterns of having been with this person in previous lifetimes.

His theory was that such connections feel 'pre-ordained' because, in fact, they are. You and Mr or Mrs Previous Lifetime are destined to keep on meeting up and working through, er, issues. Hmm. A good excuse for the non-stop bickering dynamic?

Edgar Cayce believed that the feelings aroused go instantly beyond a mere physical attraction (not that we don't love that, too) and are about the other person utterly enlivening us, physically and mentally as well as spiritually.

# Soulmating

So your soulmate is a person you're destined to be with forever and you recognize him or her right away. Other New Age theorists take that a step further. They say that we have whole soul tribes — bunches of people whom we've known before and whom our soul immediately recognizes.

Whether or not you subscribe to reincarnation dogma, something is definitely up. We do meet people we simply adore on sight! The relationship instantly feels as though we're just picking up on a conversation started elsewhere.

And, yes, this can happen with or without the sex urge — there are plenty of soulmates who are simply best friends. There are others who are lucky enough to be born equipped with soulmates in their family.

That such instant love exists — and I know for sure that it does because I knew I was going to marry my now husband the moment I saw his photograph in a magazine and experienced extreme hot and cold 'flushes' — is all the proof I need.

The story of how British actress Joanna Lumley met her husband is one of my faves and is a perfect example of 'physical impact' soulmate recognition. The Emmy Award winning star of two hit TV series, *Absolutely Fabulous* and *The New Avengers*, locked eyes with a man sitting at the church organ and was seized with the strangest sensation.

'It was like someone had pushed me sharply in the chest with a great bang,' says Joanna in her autobiography, *Stare Back and Smile* (Viking, 1989). 'I felt as though I'd had some kind of electric shock. It wasn't a matter of falling instantly in love, it was the impact of a colossal shock, completely memorable.'

The fellow who set off this reaction was Stephen Barlow. This former chorister at Canterbury Cathedral, who would become one of the world's foremost musical directors, was eight years younger than Joanna. The pair had a mutual friend at the time who lived in the country. As a 21-year-old, Joanna was staying at the friend's home when they were expecting Stephen to arrive.

'For some unknown reason, he never turned up,' says Joanna. 'I can remember feeling terribly disappointed that I wasn't going to meet this boy. But even then that struck me as odd. I was eight years older than this child and I had never met him. But the name Stephen Barlow burned into me or it came from me as though it was a memory from the future, if you can imagine something as strange as that.'

A little more than a decade later, the star was attending a marriage in the same country village. As she stepped through the porch into the church, the organist turned, looked straight at her and their eyes locked. Stephen and Joanna had finally met.

They met again in London several years later when Stephen — now 30 — was rehearsing near her home. He dropped by one day.

'Finally, we got to know each other and it became apparent, we both agreed, that it was exactly as though each of us had found our other half,' Joanna says.

The couple married in 1986 and, like so many soulmates, they are best friends who adore one another's company. They have long periods apart but they either call each other every day, or they fax one another in handwritten notes.

'With Stephen, it was not only a case of eyes meeting across a crowded room but also something deeper as well,' Joanna explains. 'An inner voice told me he was the one and when that happens you've got to go with it because your heart is open and you feel marvellous.

'If you're lucky, and I guess I am, romance continues wildly after marriage because you're wildly in love. I know that other people get bored stiff [with their marriages] and go off and have affairs. Not me, babe.'

When love walks in the door, consciousness is suddenly raised sky-high, the heart opens and you do feel marvellous, as Joanna says. You become a magical realist by default.

Soulmating is not necessarily socially convenient. Love's history is littered with unfortunate folk, cast off by those lovers

# Soulmating

who meet one another and leap heart-first into a whirl of complications and entanglements. Here is one such story.

French writer Bernard-Henri Levy first met his actress wife Arielle Dombasle when she was at one of his book-signings. She had pursued her literary hero after falling in love with his dust-jacket photo. 'It was the most moving face I had ever seen, full of pain, femininity, gravity,' Arielle says.

During a brief exchange, Arielle tried to lure Bernard-Henri into seeing a play she was appearing in. But it was Bernard-Henri who was in awe.

'I went rigid with fear,' explains Bernard-Henri. 'I said to myself, "This is impossible. She looks too bizarre, too beautiful, too this, too that." It was too dangerous, too complicated. I was thunderstruck by her beauty, her gaze, her voice, her oddness, and I didn't want to be thunderstruck — I was a libertine!'

Bernard-Henri didn't take up the offer of the play — he moved on and married another woman.

Two years later, the pair met again in Milan, Italy. In an interview with *Vanity Fair* (January 2003) Bernard-Henri said they spent the afternoon together and then the night at his hotel.

'I was bludgeoned with joy,' he says, but he also decided not to see her again (his wife had just given birth to his child).

Meanwhile, Arielle, who was also married at this stage, was holed up in her apartment, refusing to eat or to see anyone. After a month of stand-off, Bernard-Henri had to go to Italy.

'I called Arielle and she joined me in the plane, and we've been together since then,' says Bernard-Henri.

'I felt this was exactly the woman I had been waiting for, who was right for me. I understood that if I attached myself to her I would never leave her, that she would make all the others redundant, fill all the available space for passion and feelings, and that's what scared me. I didn't believe in love, did not think it existed, and if it did, that it was just an illusion, and I didn't want an illusion to be the centre of my life.'

'I feel as though I've met the one
who you think about as a child,
searching the world over and
finding the one, the right one.
I feel very blessed to have her. I feel
like I've been given my destiny.'

Actor Johnny Depp on partner, actress Vanessa Paradis

# Star-crossed lovers?

'All this time I have been thinking of nothing but you. I live only in the thought of you. I wanted to forget, to forget you. Why, oh, why, have you come?'

*The Lady With The Dog* — Anton Chekhov

# Star-crossed lovers?

I t is said of the most major love affairs in the world that they seemed meant to be or are simply 'written in the stars'. Astrology is about the Cosmic law of 'as above, so below'. This means that patterns formed by the position of the stars at our birth are akin to a celestial blueprint of our potentials in every respect. So it has always been about divining destiny and thus it is inextricably linked to the idea of fated romance.

True lovers sometimes talk of the bizarre synchronicities that brought them together — on a whim, actor Ryan Phillippe gatecrashed (his now wife) Reese Witherspoon's party. And when the magic happens, it certainly feels as though the planets have aligned in our favour.

A duo is said to be 'star-crossed' when certain astro scenarios are revealed in their respective birth charts. Astrologers look for strong soulmating indicators but simple Sun-sign compatibility (Can an Aries be happy with a Taurus? Will my Aquarius lover understand me?) is the most common and best-known use of the ancient Zodiac.

Sun-sign compatibility is basic, but it's a definite start because it shows the interaction of our core personalities.

Then, if you want a little more detail, you could check out a whole range of planetary movements that can influence your love life. For example, the Moon's contacts between your chart

# Soulmating

and another's reveal the emotional ease between you; the involvement of the Moon's Nodes is said to imply a fated aspect to a love affair; the placement of Saturn often shows whether there is a long-term potential in a structured relationship; and the planets Mars and Venus measure gung-ho sexual attraction — that sexy, little 'Hello, I love you' spark.

However, it's those dashing asteroids — Eros and Psyche — that have become most linked to soulmating and true love. Never heard of them? You soon will. They are the power players of the love game. These two are the most accurate astro indicators of our most secret selves and the soulmating potential of any relationship.

Before finding out how the asteroids Eros and Psyche affect your love life and romantic destiny, it is vital to understand the legend behind them. These asteroids were named after the eternal lovers of ancient mythology!

The story of Eros and Psyche has survived over the aeons because it strips the saga of 'us' down to the essential elements. Whether we are youthful and trembling at the threshold of first love, sophisticated and worldly, just married or gay, this tale speaks to the part of us that yearns for love and will do whatever it takes to get it...

'When you realize you want
to spend the rest of your
life with somebody, you
want the rest of your life
to start as soon as possible.'

Billy Crystal to Meg Ryan in *When Harry Met Sally*

# The legend of Eros and Psyche

'When I met him, I was definitely shocked
that I was so in love with him.'

Actress Kate Hudson on her husband, musician Chris Robinson

# The legend of Eros and Psyche

There once was a princess called Psyche. The youngest of three sisters, she is blessed with extraordinary beauty, wit and compassion. Studly suitors vie for her attention. Word of her wisdom and kindness to others spreads across the land. Her renown becomes such that the people begin to worship her in favour of Aphrodite, the goddess of love and beauty.

Peeved by this slight, Aphrodite sends her son Eros to teach Psyche a lesson. Eros, the offspring of his mother's fling with the war god Ares, is the most handsome man of all. He is the god of erotic love and his gold-tipped arrows evoke unquenchable desire in all who are struck by them.

Eros must abide by his mother's wishes and sprinkle a potion on Psyche that will make her fall in love with the ugliest man on earth. But upon seeing her, Eros becomes so overwhelmed by her beauty and sweetness that he pierces her as well as himself with one of his own arrows.

Fearful of his mother's rage, Eros flees. And when Psyche awakens she is sick with love for the beautiful boy who came to her, seemingly, in a dream. She knocks back all offers of marriage, inconsolably yearning for Eros.

In desperation, Psyche's mother, the Queen, consults an oracle who tells her that Psyche is not fated to marry a mortal. She must be left alone on top of a mountain where she is to meet her destiny. Psyche's family are convinced that she has been cursed to marry some kind of monster.

But, instead, she finds herself whisked off by the wind to a glorious palace on top of a mountain. Invisible servants waft around, ready to cater to her every whim.

Come nightfall, Eros dutifully goes to Psyche's side, declaring his love for her. He tells her that it was him she 'dreamed' of that night. He explains to her that she must never set eyes on him otherwise the spell will be broken. And if the spell was broken they would no longer be together.

And so the lovers spent night after blissful night with each other. And every night Eros would flit out of their bed before dawn to avoid being seen by Pysche. Psyche doesn't know that Eros is a god.

One evening, Psyche confides to her dream lover that she longs to see her sisters. She wants them to come to the palace to visit her. Eros prevaricates, knowing in his heart that this could wreck everything. However, he eventually relents because it upsets him to see his precious Psyche feeling so sad.

The next day the sisters arrive and are suitably impressed by the opulent palace that sits atop its own secret mountain.

However, several hours later, they become jealous of her happiness. In the pleasure gardens, they ask: 'What type of "man" is he who won't let Psyche even see his face! Don't you remember the rumoured curse? You're so naive that you're sleeping with a monster and don't even know it!'

# Soulmating

At first, Psyche argues with her sisters but, eventually, they win her over with their logic. Psyche agrees to break the rule set down by Eros. Her sisters provide her with a candle with which to see for herself the monster she loves.

That night, when Eros is sleeping, Psyche quietly sneaks off and returns with her candle aflame. Under the soft glow she sees that her lover is neither monstrous nor beastly but the man with the golden arrows — the most beautiful man in the world and the one she adores.

When the hot wax drips onto Eros's chest, he awakens in horror, knowing that the spell has been broken and their idyll of love has gone forever. He flees and Psyche faints. When she awakens, she finds herself in a barren field, alone.

Psyche is lost in the wilderness for months. Her heart is broken. One day she comes to one of the temples of Aphrodite and decides to go in and ask the love goddess for guidance.

Aphrodite eavesdrops on Psyche as she explains her story to one of her aides. She

is furious that her son has disobeyed her.
She appears before Psyche and says she
can only have her heart's desire by
completing four tasks. Psyche agrees, not
knowing that the tasks she's about to be
given are impossible...

The first task is horrendous. She must
sift through a seemingly sky-high
pile of grains — food for the sacred
doves of Aphrodite — and sort them into
different colours. The doves were suddenly
*that* discriminating! Psyche freaks out,
realizing the hopelessness of her situation.
Psyche knows all too well that Eros is the
only man she will ever love and yet she
can't have him.

An insistent voice rouses her from a fit
of despair. It's not Eros, but it's an ant sent
by him to help her. Trillions of ants work
all night to help her and, by morning,
Aphrodite is astounded — and suspicious —
to see that the impossible job is done.

The second task is worse than impossible.
It will almost certainly result in Psyche's
death! She must steal a snippet of golden
fleece from the rams of Ares, the god of

war and the father of Eros. These are no ordinary sheep but a bunch of macho beasts that charge around day and night. If she crosses their path she will be crushed.

Psyche asks them for a snippet of their fleece but they are unable to hear her amidst the thundering of their hooves. Even if they could, it is doubtful they would help. Their golden fleece is not to be given away.

Once again, Psyche is beside herself. She flops to the ground and weeps, feeling utterly lost in her despair.

A short time later, Meander, the god of rivers, appears and offers to help. He is sympathetic to lovers, having finally scored his own hard-won heart's desire, the love of a tree nymph. He points out to her that, in their excitement, the golden rams leave snags of their fleece on the low branches of the willow trees that overhang the river.

Psyche walks into the river and, as she does, Meander raises the water so that she might snatch a snippet of golden fleece.

Aphrodite is furious when she hears that Meander, her ally, has helped Pysche.

Next, Psyche is asked to fetch a cup of water from the river Styx, a river that's not under the domain of Meander. It flows from the Underworld!

Worse still, she must get the water from its source, a waterfall gushing from a rocky cliff. Even if she could climb that high, how does she bring the cup down without spilling it? She can't do it.

At that moment, a majestic eagle flies to Psyche and offers to help her. With that, the bird whisks her up to the rocky cliff, where she fills the cup, then flies her safely back down again.

From whom does this aid come? It is a mystery to Psyche.

Even Aphrodite is impressed at what Psyche has achieved. She is starting to admire this potential 'daughter-in-law'. But, she decides to set Psyche one final task before she may win Eros's love.

This time she must venture into the Underworld and bring back a sample of beauty cream from Persephone, Queen of the Underworld. Psyche knows this task is impossible — no mortal returns from here.

# Soulmating

Demeter, the fertility goddess, advises Psyche on how to approach her daughter, Persephone, a woman with her own romantic history who slowly grew to love her Underworld lord.

Unbeknown to Psyche, Eros has come to her aid. He is constantly (albeit invisibly) by Psyche's side and guides her through the murky paths to this other place.

Persephone, perhaps looking forward to her annual spring/summer sojourn in the sunlit lands above, is sympathetic to Psyche and her romantic dilemma.

She gives Psyche a pot of her special beauty cream. She also gives her permission to leave the Underworld without any hassles. But, she warns her never to open the pot of beauty cream – it would be fatal for a mortal woman to use it.

Having completed the task, Psyche begins the journey back to Aphrodite's abode to report to the goddess. She desperately yearns to be in the arms of her true love Eros.

The forthcoming reunion with Eros turns her mind's fancy to seduction but Psyche

knows that she looks a bit worse for wear.
Completing the four tasks has wreaked
havoc upon her good looks and equilibrium.
She does not yet realize that Eros loves
both the outer and inner Psyche.

Disobeying the dictum from Persephone,
Psyche opens the pot of beauty cream and
instantly falls into a deep faint. Some say
she dies at this point.

Besotted Eros flies Psyche
immediately to Zeus, the king of the
gods. Eros speaks of his love for her
so eloquently that Zeus is moved to
intervene, restore Psyche to life and make
her immortal. He then marries the couple
on the spot. And Psyche is now the
goddess of the soul.

When Aphrodite sees how happy her son
is, she softens toward the union and
indeed learns to like Psyche for herself.

Eros and Psyche live happily ever after
with their three children, aptly named
Bliss, Pleasure and Ecstasy.

# Together 4 eva

'You had me at "hello".'

Jerry (Tom Cruise) to Dorothy (Renée Zellweger) in *Jerry Maguire*

# Together 4 eva

The beating of utterly ludicrous odds in order to score true romance '4 eva' forms the basis of the greatest love stories. Never mind the tragedies such as *Romeo and Juliet*, *Antony and Cleopatra* or the thwarted romance between Rhett Butler and Scarlett O'Hara in *Gone With The Wind*.

The biggest blockbuster movies are about the love that overcomes all obstacles, including distance, war and even death itself. Think *Casablanca*, *Doctor Zhivago*, *Titanic*, *Ghost*, *Sleepless in Seattle*, *Love Story*. Even full-on action sci-fi *The Terminator* has at its core a hero who travels across time to save the woman he loves.

Real-life classic film star passion? Katharine Hepburn and Spencer Tracy, Elizabeth Taylor and Richard Burton (they were married twice to each other), Humphrey Bogart and Lauren Bacall.

'How can one change one's entire life and build a new life on a moment of love?' asks Greta Garbo as Marguerite in *Camille*. 'And yet, that's what you make me want to close my eyes and do,' she says to her lover Armand. How indeed? It's a similar dilemma to that of Psyche.

The legend of Eros and Psyche is the original version. Over the centuries, it has naturally been analyzed non-stop. Mythology historian H A Guerber says that Eros is the Sun God seeking in Psyche the Goddess of the Dawn. So Eros can't rise to

# Soulmating

full light without her. He can't even really be. And without the light of Eros to shine upon her inner beauty, Psyche can't be complete. Each needs the other and, unlike the players in many a myth, they wind up happy ever after.

The story of Eros and Psyche is clearly about the manifestation of true love after trial and tribulation, the struggle to become the 'other half' and the certainty that people who have found their soulmate can act in ways that make absolutely no sense to those around them.

Psyche also does most of the work in this myth so it is more the female's journey toward love than the male's. But, really, it's about the metamorphosis evoked by love.

The sisters who insist that Psyche is sleeping with a monster may have a point, from their perspective. Yet does real love require a second opinion? Our heroine risks her own true love by trusting the lights of those who are not in love!

In darker versions of this myth, Psyche goes off and sleeps with a few monsters before discovering Eros. Ahem! Who among us can relate?

You could say that the helpful eagle character is lofty perspective and scoring some golden fleece under difficult conditions is about subverting male systems with sneakiness. Maybe the sorting of the grain is to do with engaging our logical 'ant mind' to sift through the received opinion that so often comes between us and our emotions?

Could the beauty cream picked up in the Underworld be a metaphor for the knowing radiance to be gained — afterwards, of course — from a vile relationship?

Whatever we take from the legend of Eros and Psyche, it is undeniably a wonderful love story as well as an allegory for our own progress toward love serenity.

'I really wasn't meant to be at the dinner but destiny lured me there. Justin was flirting with my girlfriend at the other end of the table, and when he came to sit next to me, I reacted really badly. We were fighting for the next two hours, screaming at each other. He was drunk. I was drunk and everyone was laughing. His best friend said: "Look, Justin's found his wife"!'

Model Natalia Vodianova on meeting her husband, artist Justin Portman

His view on the relationship? 'I think we've been married from the moment we met.'

# Soulmating a go-go: the how-to of love witchery

'Medicine, law, business, engineering, these are noble pursuits and necessary to sustain life. But poetry, beauty, romance, love, these are what we stay alive for.'

Teacher John Keating (Robin Williams) in *Dead Poets Society*

# Soulmating a go-go: the how-to of love witchery

You don't need to be a scientist, doctor, shrink or a spacey New Ager to discover the secrets to soulmating, compatibility and true love. Anyone can do it. It's that easy. All you need is a birthday.

The great thing about the Eros and Psyche signs is that they can tell you a whole lot about your love life — like who is your ideal man or woman, how your partner really feels about you and what type of person makes the better soulmate for you. This is 'personalized' soulmating at its best. It's a fast-track to finding true love and it eliminates all that time-consuming guesswork.

At the back of this book are the astrological tables (ephemerides) of Eros and Psyche. The tables tell you the astrological sign that these two were in for any date of birth.

Here's how to get started. You first look up the date of birth of you and your partner in each of the tables. This will tell you what Sun sign Eros and Psyche were in at the time of your birth. Once you're done deciphering the romantic soul secrets they reveal, you can start cross-referencing via the Soulmating maps on pages 154 and 156 to discover the compatibility of a relationship via Eros and Psyche.

Let's say you're a girl with the hugest crush in the world on Mr Maybe. You look up your Eros sign to find out the kind of guy you really need, like it or not! Then, for an insight into Inner

# Soulmating

You — your secret (soul-driven!) romantic persona, look up your Psyche sign to see what you're really all about.

Now comes the love-witchery part, the bit of the book that enables you to seemingly get inside the head of Mr Maybe, wowing him even more than you probably already have.

You look up his Eros sign and get a full-on glimpse of his secret lover-boy self. Hmmm? Interesting? Then you can discover his Psyche sign, the truest astro indicator of his ideal woman.

Mr Maybe? Or Mr Forever? Now that you know him (and yourself) a little better, why not see how your Eros and Psyche signs get along? Check out His Eros with Her Psyche and Her Eros with His Psyche. Follow the symbols to read the two soulmating interpretations. Why two? Because, believe it or not, in the magical astro world, these two are always in relation to one another. Looking up (say) only his Eros with your Psyche will give you just half of the picture.

When in complete harmony, Eros and Psyche add up to fated love. That's right! If you believe in the previous lifetimes paradigm, it's a definite indicator that this full-on-feeling dynamic is actually a reunion of two lovers who have already known one another ... before.

Let's examine the secret personas and soulmating potential of two major celebs, just to make sure you're on the right track.

Bodacious Ben Affleck was born on 15 August, 1972. On the face of it he is a strong and egomaniacal Leo. This is so fitting for a latter-day matinee idol whose presence can 'open' a movie. However, when we look further, we see that his Eros is in Pisces. His secret 'lover-boy' self is akin to Prince Charming, burdened — bless him — with romantic idealism that few real-life relationships can live up to.

Cool. But Ben's Psyche, which reveals his ideal woman, is in Virgo! So he's a discriminating fusspot, judging every detail about his girl. Compare the Eros and Psyche signs of this guy and you wind up with someone who wants to enjoy unconditional love

# Soulmating a go-go: the how-to of love witchery

from a super-control-freaking perfectionist. Maybe he and Jennifer Lopez make sense after all! Let's check her out.

Another multitalented Leo, she was born on 27 July, 1970. So her Eros (which reveals her ideal man) is in Capricorn (for Jennifer, it really *is* about the money, honey, along with a hefty dose of status and prestige) whilst her Psyche (which reveals her secret romantic persona) is in Gemini. She's just so-o-o fickle and yet demanding!

Now for this couple's soulmating potential. Looking at the ephemeris, we see that matching his Psyche in Virgo with her Eros in Capricorn makes this a diamond relationship — classic love at first sight sizzling between two superstars. Her Eros and his Psyche are symbolized by the Sun. This means they will always be able to renew their love. Even if they're split up, they'll remain friends. Neither of them will want to be the one who loves less (or more!) for one second. It has to be utterly equal so let the psychodrama begin! Could this be you and your love? Or are you the slow-burn, long-haul 'love that dare not speak its name' type of love affair?

Now you can investigate you and yours! Or amaze friends with your astro-analyst soulmating skills and even make astounding celebrity love predictions!

Happy soulmating!

# His Eros reveals ...
# his secret
# lover-boy self!

'You cannot think how my feelings are
alive toward you, probably more than ever
and they never can be diminished.'

Lord Horatio Nelson, in a letter written to his lover, Lady Emma Hamilton

# His Eros reveals ... his secret lover-boy self!

I n astrology, Eros represents the smitten heart. The Eros sign of a man shows us how he truly wants to be in love. It's like the 'in his dreams' best romantic expression of himself.

By tuning into this particular persona — which he may not be that consciously aware of himself — you effortlessly access an off-limits area of his mind and heart.

It's an aspect of his male identity that may not even have been awakened yet. Yet, like the Eros of myth, he can only rise and shine via the expression of his Eros sign.

Even the most callow boy or hardcore womanizer (perhaps especially him!) has a secret fantasy guy hiding inside. Understanding his Eros personality takes you beyond the realms of Sun sign astrology.

It's great that he is (say) a suave Libran but if it's romance you're after, you'll get where you want a lot quicker by relating to his (for example) conspiracy theorizing and intensity-craving Eros in Scorpio!

Real-life celeb example? Colin Farrell. This guy's a Gemini and sure lives it up like one. However, despite the wild partying et al, he's already a dad and seems most truly happy in this role. His Eros is in solid Taurus and he has Psyche in clucky Cancer. To put it really simply, play to his Eros sign and he will feel truly understood, fully a man. Wanna know it? Read on!

# His Eros is in...

'Her face
so fair
first bent
mine eye

Her tongue
so sweet
then drew
mine ear

Her wit
so sharp
then hit
my heart.'

*Her Face* — Sir Arthur Gorges

'We met at my 21st birthday party, and we immediately hit it off. But he left the next day and was gone for two months. So we wrote each other letters and really got to know each other more through correspondence and talking on the telephone than any sort of physical attraction. It was so romantic; he wrote me these wonderful letters. And, after he came back, it was like we were an old married couple. We were so comfortable with each other. I really believe I was meant to find this person in my life, and he was meant to find me, and we were meant to be together. I feel very corny talking about it, but I am just overwhelmed with a sense that it chose us; we didn't choose it.'

Actress Reese Witherspoon on meeting her husband,
actor Ryan Phillippe

# Aries

## March 21 - April 20

Cosmically activated by the scent of ginseng and musk, 'sporty' fragrances, even sweat. He loves it that you appreciate his au naturel reek. To trigger his Eros, lay it on thick.

He wants to hear: Save me!

He is love's daredevil. In his mind, he gallivants around Camelot, the bravest knight of all and official rescuer of distressed damsels. He needs a quest to motivate him. His gigantic ego won't let him admit it but he wants to work in scoring your unconditional love. Give him the chase that he craves and somehow forget to call it off. Even if you've been blissfully bonded together for 20 years, Eros in Aries is mission-oriented. Engage his protective instincts with a 'he did me wrong' tale of woe ... he likes to shine in comparison with other lesser males.

Richard Burton, Ewan McGregor, Kid Rock

# Taurus

## April 21- May 21

Cosmically activated by the smell of freshly cut grass and any similar fragrance. Woo him in the wilderness, walk through a field. The term 'roll in the hay' was invented for this guy.

He wants to hear: I'm yours

A stayer, Eros in Taurus most values sensual compatibility. Seemingly insatiable, he is best won via bedwork and appeals to his so-tactile nature. Once truly in love, he is possessive, doting and demanding, lavishing his lover with athletic devotion. Despite an often-intense, sexing-it-up phase in youth, he yearns to be placed on a perfect husbandly pedestal. His libido waxes rather than wanes with a long-term love affair. Stability really turns him on ... he sees soulmating not as metaphysical but as metabolic, part of his very physical being.

Russell Crowe, Colin Farrell

# Gemini

## May 22 - June 21

Cosmically activated by ever changing scents.
He always likes to be surprised. Flip him out
with a hot Latin scent one moment, then blast
him with a fresh, clean soap smell the next.

He wants to hear: Come here, go away!

The laughing cavalier of love, Eros in Gemini can't engage his heart without a strong mental affinity. He's aroused by new info, gossip and jokes that he hasn't heard yet. He gets bored with moralizing and emotive ranting. So just keep him interested with lots of chitchat. He'll love that you change the subject before he can. Whether he's happily soulmated or not, this guy needs to feel as though he's with a variety of people. Feel free to show off the myriad aspects of beautiful you to him. Reassure him by remaining unpredictable and always elusive.

Antonio Banderas, Colin Firth, Hugh Grant, Ryan Phillippe

# Cancer

## June 22 - July 23

Cosmically activated by scents that remind him
of Mama, whether he admits or not. If in doubt,
always go mega-girly and classic. He's lured by
the odour of a time past that maybe never was.


He wants to hear: Hold me!

He is the prince of tides, a mood-swinger and manipulator of hearts. He's easily enslaved by sentimental gestures. Tread tenderly around anything to do with Mama. The way to his heart really is through his stomach — or massage. Bored by trivia but blessed with granite strength and serenity for real challenges, Eros in Cancer really understands the feminine mind. Accustomed from birth to gaga-gushing attention from females, beauty moves him. He abhors sleaze and vulgarity and will not be remotely amused by coarse stories.

Matt Drudge, Guy Pearce, Gavin Rossdale

# Leo

## July 24 - August 23

Cosmically activated by officially difficult Diva
scents. He likes a luxury brand fully layered via
the trappings of body and bath versions. He just
loves a smell that says, 'Hello, I am here'.

He wants to hear: I love the real you,
beneath the fame

The sultan of love, Eros in Leo wants unconditional worship. Non-stop sycophancy is an optional extra. His heart is gracious, regal and giving if perhaps too easily ensnared by hardcore glamour. Like Eros in Aries, he appreciates the chase aspect of romance but with added theatrics. He gets off on the grand gesture. For example, the ritual destruction of love letters from past suitors is now rendered irrelevant. His fantasy of true romance can be annihilated by the split ends of everyday life. Don't undermine his dignity. The queen of his heart must act the part.

David Arquette, Pete Sampras, Justin Theroux

# Virgo

## August 24 - September 23

Cosmically activated by clean, clean, clean.
Loves the pure smell of soap, freshly scrubbed
skin and recently washed hair. The Virgo Eros is
utterly freaked out by OTT scents.

He wants to hear: I trust you

Eros in Virgo equals love in observation mode. He has a details fetish so he relishes every little titbit of info on his object of desire. He likes to be taken into your confidence. He loves that you ask for his advice. Mystery is not a major turn-on. He wants a companion. But Eros in Virgo comes with a strong moral kick and a code of correctness. He'll happily sit and listen to you whinge about work, talk about your technique for making toast — whatever. But he'll flip out big time at any hint of dishonesty or tacky conduct.

David Beckham, Enrique Iglesias, Prince William, Luke Wilson

# Libra

## September 24 - October 23

Cosmically activated by classic florals. He has a
highly discerning sense of smell and hates tricky
fragrances, synthetics and over-application. He
could easily have a fetish about body lotion
or scented lipgloss.

He wants to hear: You are so beautiful

Eros in Libra fantasizes about a total merger of heart, mind, body and soul. Once soulmated, he gets off on non-stop togetherness. His romantic ideals are lofty. A relationship should be nothing less than poetry in motion. He can be enraptured by the idea of woman — adoring of the concept, less taken with the everyday reality. A natural-born aesthete, he thrills to beauty, philosophy and talent but is appalled by banality. Keep it real? No way. Make it surreal. The elegant euphemism is preferable to au naturel.

Edward Burns, Tobey Maguire, Adam Sandler

# Scorpio

## October 24 - November 22

Cosmically activated by the smell of you,
genuinely. For example, daub some 'body fluid'
behind your ears. He likes pure essential oils
[not cheap fakes] and is a secret admirer of musk.

He wants to hear: Wow! how do you know that?

Eros in Scorpio loves on two different levels. The first is dalliance — he has an enormous capacity to fool around without his hard-to-get heart even being involved. The second is true romance, which he is wary of, knowing his capacity for deep involvement. This man harbours unbelievable depths of emotion. He secretly reveres the concept of his Twin Soul but is also a game player, stopping only with the woman secure enough to call his bluff. He fantasizes about the grand passion that is strong enough to linger for lifetimes.

David Bowie, George Clooney,
Ralph Fiennes, Ian Somerhalder

# Sagittarius

## November 23 - December 21

Cosmically activated by the smell of something sporty such as liniment. If he isn't into the locker room scene he may instead crave something spearminty. Think grassy or fresh.

He wants to hear: Don't fence me in!

The philosopher of love, Eros in Saggo craves candour. Incapable of sneaky behaviour or mind games, he likes to express feelings freely, on his terms and in an expansive context. He sees love as a trip and this guy is an inveterate traveller. He loves the idea of two total individuals together on the same journey. His heart engages only after a fun and life-enhancing friendship has been established. He likes to hear you say 'come away with me'. Romance is his escape and not a necessary component of mundane life.

Jake Gyllenhaal, Hugh Jackman, Prince Harry, Will Smith, James Van Der Beek

# Capricorn

## December 22 - January 20

Cosmically activated by the sweet smell of
success. He likes the whole package to be clean
like Virgo and non-vulgar like Leo, but so
understated like the faint waft of
professionally blow-dried hair.

He wants to hear: Financial independence
turns me on

The player of love treats romance with respect. Whether he lets on to her or not, he is auditioning applicants for the position of life partner. Eros in Capricorn is into strategic courtship. Watch for his *Princess and the Pea*-style tests. Worldly and assured, he's after a liaison that not only fulfils his lusty sensual requirements but is mutually supportive. His true soulmate is, above all else, appropriate to where he feels he is heading in life. Chaos tempts him not. He loves the idea of the couple that schemes together to rise above, becoming more than the sum of their parts.

Christian Bale, Matt Damon, Ethan Hawke, Owen Wilson

# Aquarius

## January 21 - February 19

Cosmically activated by the weird fragrances, the avant-garde, hard-to-find scents that are talking points in themselves. Eros in Aqua loves metallic and/or fruity fragrances.

He wants to hear: You're not like the other guys

Socially progressive, Eros in Aquarius believes in love Utopia. He can appear unfeeling because his romantic ideals involve mind enmeshment. His heart only softens with intellectual equality. He is capable of playing loyalty-testing games to ensure that he is able to let his guard down. The cant of romance bores him senseless. Eros in Aquarius can forget your birthday, let alone love anniversaries, but show the deepest tenderness in unexpected ways. He is easily bored with social convention — drive him away quickly by making such obligations an essential part of your relationship.

Johnny Depp, Heath Ledger, Brad Pitt

# Pisces

## February 20 - March 20

Cosmically activated by ylang- ylang essential
oil. Unlike most men, Eros in Pisces is
interested in complexity and mystery. If in
doubt, try anything that's oriental. But, make
sure you use it sparingly.

He wants to hear: I'm so in love with you

Eros in Pisces is the king of love and is the most romantic sign of all. He yearns for the all-enveloping romance, one that annihilates walls between the lovers and fulfils his childhood dreams of The One. This man is capable of unconditional love and acceptance. Wildly compassionate, he can't fall truly in love with a woman who's mean-hearted. Cynical arrangements or the merely 'convenient' relationship harden his heart. Yet, because he believes so utterly in love, he can easily be hurt by those who fail to grasp his inner goodness.

Ben Affleck, Matthew Broderick, Jude Law, Sam Mendes, Freddie Prinze Jr, Ben Stiller

# Her Psyche reveals... her romantic persona

'She croons, like a cat to its claws;
Cries, "I'm old enough to live
And delight in a lover's praise,
Yet keep to myself my own mind;
I dance to the right, to the left;
My luck raises the wind."

"Write all my whispers down,"
She cries to her true love.
"I believe, I believe, in the moon! –
What weather of heaven is this?"

"The storm, the storm of a kiss."'

*Her Words* – Theodore Roethke

# Her Psyche reveals ... her romantic persona

The sign of a woman's Psyche reveals her inner 'girlish' emotions regarding romance. It is here she shows off her secret self. Her Psyche sign may be the same as her Sun sign, in which case the search for true love is likely to be an integral part of her life. Or it could represent a hidden aspect of the self — an aspect that a woman most needs to have accepted.

In fact, a woman's Psyche sign — the planet in which she has Psyche — is often an accurate indicator of the dreams she abandoned at puberty, a 'self' that was covered over in childhood or a deeper yearning of the soul that she has decided to hide.

So expressing her Psyche sign will always provide peace of heart for a woman. When she is soulmated, it allows the perfect excuse to let that spirit run free. Romance will never fully work if the Psyche sign is somehow unable to shine.

This is where soulmating and its indicators, Eros and Psyche, are so powerful for women. A partner who sincerely desires that a whole part of a woman be repressed to fit his fantasy is not The One. He's also not the one who disrespects her dreams and achievements or who subtly undermines her by insisting that she dress in a particular way.

When a woman's Psyche is evoked she feels as if something from long ago is unfurling within her. It often materializes as an almost pre-adolescent feeling, akin to that first flush of love before sex got involved in the scenario. It is as if, no matter what the usual trials of love, she feels finally free to be herself.

The word Psyche means both soul and butterfly and so, along with being the goddess of the soul, she also represents our little flitting dreams of romance, freed from the drab chrysalis at last.

When a woman's Psyche is triggered, it's as though a light has been switched on inside her. Whether it is a new lover or simply the discovery of a new best friend, that inner glow is probably the expression of the true self.

# Her Psyche is in...

'I thought this was probably an illusion
that was going to go away. But, it didn't.
We started calling each other, then we saw
each other, and I realized that I was in love.'

Actor Antonio Banderas on his wife, actress Melanie Griffith

'St Antony's Dance: fell down the steps, and seem to have fallen in love with J. We didn't dance much.'

Novelist Iris Murdoch's diary entry for 3 June, 1954

'We talked without stopping, endless, childish chatter, seeming to invent on the spot, as we talked, a whole infantile language of our own.'

Her husband John Bayley's version of the encounter

# Aries

## March 21 - April 20

Cosmically activated by crimson flowers of all types like roses, tulips, gerberas. She likes anything that's boldly burgundy. With her, you should say it large, say it with scarlet.

She needs to know that she is feminine

Psyche in Aries is the warrior queen. Headstrong, a thrill-seeker and imbued with a strong sense of entitlement, she charges young into romance. The initial approach to love is combative and her high demands scare many men off. Psyche in Aries can be too strong, sticking in a vile relationship because she is 'not a wimp'. Truly in love, she learns that a love affair need not involve a constant power struggle. She needs, more than most, someone exciting and 'tough' enough to earn her respect but who is also tender with her well-concealed dreams of love.

Naomi Campbell, Uma Thurman

# Taurus

## April 21 - May 21

Cosmically activated by wildflowers gathered
just for her. Try dandelions, moss, herbs,
flowers with therapeutic meaning.
The ultimate? Something you've grown yourself
or perhaps something you can drink?


She needs to know that her allure is working

Psyche in Taurus is the natural born seductress who trusts her sensual instincts above all. Her vital indicators of love are the scent of her mate and pleasurable skin-to-skin contact. However, if the fingertips don't zing off one another at first touch, she turns off. Flighty, on-off-on-again guys need not apply. However, these types will still swarm around her, longing to be soothed by that grounded aura. A true sybarite, she is drawn to abundance. Nature and stability of affection evoke her deep inner serenity.

Liz Hurley, Iman, Angelina Jolie, Jennifer Lopez, Kristin Scott Thomas, Brooke Shields

# Gemini

## May 22 - June 21

Cosmically activated by a surprise posy. She
officially thinks flowers are a cheap romantic
trick. But, if you pull out the totally unexpected,
for-no-reason bouquet, she melts.

She needs to know that she will be amused

The muse of love and a sparkling wit, she is able to spin the mundane into sparkling fresh vistas. Psyche in Gemini is comfortable with romantic ambiguity to the point of perhaps even preferring it. She trusts her mind, staying where the stimulation is, needing both to amuse and be amused. Her romantic ideal is to be a co-conspirator in love, the true companion and confidante of her soulmate. She quickly realizes that Mr (You-Figure-It-Out) Taciturn is not for her. Complex and beguiling, she is literally terrified of dull people.

Christina Aguilera, Jennifer Connelly, Danielle Spencer, Charlize Theron, Shania Twain, Rachel Weisz, Reese Witherspoon

# Cancer

## June 22 - July 23

Cosmically activated by waterlilies. To trigger
the nurturing but complex depths of the
Cancerian Psyche, bring anything that grows in
the water, or November lilies. Think lush.

She needs to know that she is safe

She is the empress of hearts, a woman of profound nurturing instincts and compassion. Some wince at the 'lame duck' guy — she sees only the swan-in-waiting. Her all-understanding mien attracts many not-so-suitable suitors. Spookily, she is able to morph into whatever guise feels most appropriate for the circumstances. Yet this Psyche must take care to stay attuned to her own true needs and avoid wandering around lost in the desire-driven projections of others. Highly emotional and intuitive, she needs a lover to cherish her extreme sensitivities.

Natalie Portman, Princess Diana

# Leo

## July 24 - August 23

Cosmically activated by yellow flowers such as
sunflowers, marigolds, daffodils, yellow roses.
The Psyche in Leo girl is at the centre of her
universe. Maybe the Sun Goddess rose...

She needs to know that she is the star

Psyche in Leo is the showgirl at heart, needing admiration from more than just one-quarter of the male population for true happiness. A born creative spirit, she flees fast from mediocrity. She makes men giddy and she fancies the idea of being dizzy with love. The first moments of a crush are heaven for Psyche in Leo. But herein lies the problem. She craves a love beyond all others, the greatest love show on earth. But what relationship can actually live up to that? Easily bedazzled by good looks, her heart's true fulfilment lies in manifesting her own star quality.

Beyoncé Knowles, Jada Pinkett Smith

# Virgo

## August 24 - September 23

Cosmically activated by rushes, river grasses, or one of those lettuce arrangements. She likes anything that's green. Her vampish knowingness and grasp of nuance suggest an arrangement of kale with sword ferns.

She needs to know that it's more than good sex

Psyche in Virgo is the vamp of love and the mistress of nuance. Whatever her lover's unspoken fantasies or secret motivations, she's onto it. She's slinky, suave and so totally together that it's holistic. But Psyche in Virgo frets, yearning for someone to show the same grasp of her details. She wants to be finessed, to have someone remember her favourite poem or the thread of the conversation from three months ago. Utterly sensual, she is nonetheless most enticed by a deep mental affinity, by someone who understands her with no explanations needed.

Pamela Anderson, Kirsten Dunst,
Sarah Michelle Gellar, Melanie Griffith,
Jade Jagger, Nicole Kidman,
Sarah Jessica Parker, Meg Ryan,
Britney Spears, Elizabeth Taylor, Liv Tyler

# Libra

## September 24 - October 23

Cosmically activated by pink flowers. The
Psyche in Libra woman is girl-girly in love and
she prefers subtle shades. Think pink: fuchsias,
pink gerberas, coral carnations.

She needs to know that she will be allowed
to breathe

Psyche in Libra is the dream girl of many but her own heart remains somehow detached – a skilful romantic player but somehow disengaged from the action. So sophisticated in the arts of love, she is also too smart for many of her would-be lovers. The Libran Psyche requires someone with her own depth of sophistication and worldliness. She can't handle too much emotional intensity or someone who sees a relationship as simply a socially convenient unit. Rife with ambiguity, she wants to be doted upon, yet at the same time afforded her precious personal space.

Cameron Diaz, Brittany Murphy,
Gwyneth Paltrow, Rachel Ward

# Scorpio

## October 24 - November 22

Cosmically activated by something growing. It has to be viable, alive and a bit different from the run of the mill. A cactus? A feng shui money plant? She also has a soft spot for berries.

She needs to know that she will not be lied to

The enchantress of love, Psyche in Scorpio is a strategist. Preferring to bewitch rather than be bedazzled, she moves in quietly and presents herself in many different guises. Her ultimate love goal is the 'nothing but you' paradigm. Should she be involved in a mere fling, her standards are almost impossible for anyone to live up to. She is a super control freak, running the dalliance on her terms, like it or not. The lover who betrays her trust to even the teeniest degree is out that door, forgotten in a moment. She knows her journey is to find The One.

Ashley Judd, Madonna, Vanessa Paradis, Audrey Tautou, Naomi Watts

# Sagittarius

## November 23 - December 21

Cosmically activated by plants that make a
political statement. She loves natives, especially
the ones that have been ousted by exotics over
the years. She adores the eco dimension.

She needs to know that she will not be forced to
be someone else

Psyche in Saggo is the adventuress, the most free-spirited lover of all. She is at her most ecstatic during a 'You understand me, you really do!' moment with a new love interest. In her soul she is a child at play in the sometimes too-grown-up world of adult relationships. There is always a wild child in the heart of this woman. She would throw over a sensible liaison in two seconds — even if only in her mind — just to experience the bliss of the moment. No matter how fixed her reality, her heart may only be unlocked by a fellow visionary wanderer.

Helena Christensen, Catherine Deneuve

# Capricorn

## December 22 - January 20

Cosmically activated by a mauve journey of status. Psyche in Cap is switched on by nature's finest like orchids, tulips and dahlias ... but not in red. Stay elegant and stick to lavender.

She needs to know that she is The Trophy

Worldly and assured, Psyche in Capricorn is the prima diva of love. A true trophy bride for a hero, she is adept at scoring the guy that no-one else can get. Until Mr Perfect comes along, her heart is often a no-fly zone. Her secret soul is well enclosed, protecting her from exploitation. Mature love often becomes her more than the games of early youth, where her gifts can be overshadowed by some tougher competition. She is a work-in-progress, learning from life as she goes along, honing her extreme sensuality and insight.

Jennifer Aniston, Fanny Ardant,
Jennifer Love Hewitt, Kate Moss,
Mena Suvari, Christy Turlington

# Aquarius

## January 21 - February 19

Cosmically activated by the Zen approach.
Psyche in Aqua leans heavily to the simple yet
powerful. Think bamboo, ikebana ... but not
bonsai. Watch her thrill to the perfect origami.

She needs to know this is for real

From an early age, Psyche in Aquarius knows that she is unconventional in love. The druidess of romance, she is euphorically independent, unwilling to be 'grounded' by any but the most ideal of men. The source of her power lies in her refusal to be anyone but her authentic self. Her dream relationship is a true companionship, mutually supportive beyond the dreams of most love affairs. Breathtakingly frank, she has no time for playing games and typical romantic cant. Her only true love is the man strong enough to let her be her utterly complicated self.

Victoria Beckham, Claire Danes, Kate Hudson, Jewel, Elle Macpherson, Pink, Hilary Swank, Catherine Zeta-Jones

# Pisces

## February 20 - March 20

Cosmically activated by white flowers. Whether they're conspicuous gardenias, sexy jasmine or mysterious Apache plumes, this girl adores the intricate scent of such blooms.

She needs to know that her sensitive side is also acknowledged

Jaded as she may pretend to be, Psyche in Pisces is love's princess, the most romantic of them all. This is a woman who never gives up on her girlhood dreams of true love. Compassionate and blessed with the magic gift of being able to love unconditionally, her kindness can lead her up many a wrong track. Underestimate this woman at your peril. She likes to project vulnerability but is actually the Psyche sign most capable of reinvention. She needs a lover sensitive enough to see beyond the myriad personae that she tries on for fun and to nurture the sweet 'child' within.

Drew Barrymore, Natalie Imbruglia

# His Psyche reveals...
# what he wants in a woman

Arwen: 'Do you remember the time when we first met?'
Aragorn: 'I thought I had strayed into a dream.'

from the film *The Lord of the Rings, The Fellowship of the Ring*

# His Psyche reveals ... what he wants in a woman

There are many ways to a man's heart. One of them is investigating his Psyche sign as it will reveal his secret ideal woman. A man's Psyche sign operates on a more clandestine level than a Sun sign. Even though it signifies the kind of female energy he needs in order to feel truly fulfilled, his Psyche could be operating subconsciously, lost beneath the roar of a full-on planet like Mars.

Interestingly, actors Catherine Zeta-Jones and Michael Douglas have their Psyches exactly in conjunct. This means that her innermost femininity matches his female ideal. The acting duos of Ben Affleck and Jennifer Lopez and Sarah Jessica Parker and Matthew Broderick also have strong Psyche-Psyche links.

When a man meets a woman who sets off his Psyche energy he feels instantly liberated. He also senses immediately that this is going to be a huge relationship. His romantic and protective instincts can't help but be awakened. He becomes the best version of himself that he can be, leaving old flames astounded.

How many times have you heard the tale of the girl who apparently 'tamed' some bad boy? Nobody can believe how the one-time heartbreaker is now swooning around. The reason? His Psyche has been activated.

The Eros-Psyche phenomenon is so strong that it doesn't have to be an exact Eros-Psyche link. A Psyche-Psyche link, or even a woman's Sun sign being in the same sign as his Psyche, can't help but evoke love.

So, yeah! Another little bit of secret astro biz! If your Psyche sign is the same as his Sun sign — whoah! But just getting his Psyche sign is a valuable insight into his inner feminine ideal.

# His Psyche is in...

'You must allow me to tell you how ardently I admire
and love you.'

Mr Darcy to Elizabeth in *Pride and Prejudice* — Jane Austen

'It was quite shocking to me to
fall in love. I was completely
not beyond having an affair.
I thought that was a great idea.
But falling in love? I didn't
see it coming at all. I thought,
"This is fun", and then, bam!'

Actress Uma Thurman on her partner, actor Ethan Hawke

# Aries

## March 21 - April 20

Cosmically activated by a powerful bass riff. He turns onto music via the beat and this is the way to his heart. He knows how to vibe in a sophisticated way, but he's a closet metal-head.

He needs to know that he will not be lied to

His dream girl isn't even a girl – she's a dominatrix. This guy is fearless and in no way intimidated by the strong female dynamic. He is confident enough about his masculinity to flip things around and become playful or even passive if he feels like it. He falls for women other men would consider officially difficult. This man is not remotely threatened by her success, opinions or charisma. But he can't bear to be lied to and will always honour his lover's candour. He loves the energetic and positive woman.

David Beckham, Enrique Iglesias

# Taurus

## April 21- May 21

Cosmically activated by the music of his youth.
The Psyche in Taurus man lives in a world of
how things should be. He needs you to totally
'get' the tunes he is most loyal to.

He needs to know that frequent sex is not an issue

P syche in Taurus is the guy in love with a figment. Okay, a time-tested classic ideal of beauty and femininity. He secretly yearns for the swimsuit-model type who'll cook him a carb-loaded dinner or the mogul woman, wealthy in her own right but who trusts his financial advice. Yes, it's tricky, all right, but easier to handle once you remember that he's enraptured by his sensual urges, an utter lover of beauty and aesthetics. No matter what his prowling habits, he longs for a settled and stable love existence. Once he is taken, he rarely gazes into other pastures.

Joshua Leonard, Tobey Maguire, Scott Major

# Gemini

## May 22 - June 21

Cosmically activated by whatever he has not heard before. Don't bother this guy with songs of meaning, just amaze him with something gimmicky. With his fickleness, he loves compilation albums.

He needs to know that change is okay

The guy with Psyche in Gemini will put up with sly and fickle vixenly types. Actually, he prefers it that way. If a woman wants to mess with this guy's mind he tells them to go ahead. He loves it. In fact, without a willing partner in his innuendo, wit and sibling-combative-banter games, this love affair won't even begin. A variety buff, his true love is a multifaceted minx-witch type, never the same persona for two days running. His true love is complicated. However, she is neither boring nor a whiner nor into making turgid emotional demands. Remember, his Psyche is symbolized by The Twins.

Antonio Banderas, Matt Damon, Colin Firth, Hugh Grant, Jake Gyllenhaal, Ethan Hawke, Ewan McGregor, Ben Stiller

# Cancer

## June 22 - July 23

Cosmically activated by emotive music. It could be classical or New Age, perhaps Ennio Morricone. What does it for Psyche in Cancer is a musical piece from their belle époque.

He needs to know there's a safe place for his feelings

The sign of Cancer is linked to the goddess Psyche, so the man with Psyche in Cancer seems to have a direct line into the female soul. Combine that with his deep subconscious drive for total security — that is, back to the womb — and he can be the classic womanizer. His relationship with his mother or a key maternal figure is intensely important and provides the key to his romantic self-expression. His feminine ideal is totally womanly, soft and giving. She is a natural-born nurturer of both children and animals, a total girl's girl and spontaneously artistic or creative.

George Clooney, John Cusack, Colin Farrell

# Leo

## July 24 - August 23

Cosmically activated by glitzy music. He may
have a secret collection of songs from the New
Romantic period. Or he adores OTT pomp like
the *1812 Overture*. Make sure it's grand.

He needs to know that everyone else wanted her

His inner ideal of the ultimate woman is a superstar — gorgeous, acclaimed and his. The man with Psyche in Leo fantasizes about — or has! — a life of success and luxury of which his woman is one of the most important indicators. He likes the glitz, glam and psychodrama of love, someone who is a personage in her own right, a prima diva by nature and yet also warm, generous and talented. Frankly, he needs to feel that she is an 'object' of some worth and status. His Inspiration is old Hollywood movies. Think golden, think bombshell.

Pete Sampras, Adam Sandler, Luke Wilson

# Virgo

## August 24 - September 23

Cosmically activated by clever, even difficult music. Don't think that just because he's into jazz, it means he wants to dance. When he says 'jazz' he means goatees and berets.

He needs to know that details count
for something

The man with Psyche in Virgo longs for someone to understand him on every level. But this trick must somehow be accomplished with a high degree of sophistication. He loves the woman who can draw an intelligent conclusion without him having to spell things out. His Ms Ideal is meticulous without making a big fuss of it, and someone who is together, worldly and witty. Eschewing mess and living an out-there lifestyle, she is clean-living and discreet. Intensely moral, Psyche in Virgo appreciates a 'good' woman who respects his need for privacy.

Ben Affleck, Matthew Broderick, James Van Der Beek, Prince William

# Libra

## September 24 - October 23

Cosmically activated by elegant quartets and beautiful singing. Gorgeous music is perfect for the Psyche in Libra; it reaffirms his love of beauty while letting him stay distant.

He needs to know that she is a mystery

Psyche in Libra likes mysterious beauties. Familiarity can create contempt with this guy and perhaps the next step is longing for new stimuli. He can wind up in love with the general concept of 'woman' but, really, he is ducking the challenge of true romance. His other method for avoiding the nitty-gritty of reality? Being madly in love with another man's woman. If her situation changes he may lose interest faster than he loses her phone number. His feminine ideal is lovely, supernaturally elegant and smart. She stays forever just a few steps in front of him, creating that elusive quality he prizes so highly.

Guy Pearce, Gavin Rossdale

# Scorpio

## October 24 - November 22

Cosmically activated by intense, brooding pieces with eerie instrumentals or featuring depressing 'poetry'. He often selects his music based on how the musician lived ... or died.

He needs to know why another man's photo is in her wallet

Bring it on! Psyche in Scorpio engenders the man who is ready for the big challenges. His ideal woman is intense, complicated and difficult. He can be the biggest womanizer on earth but, secretly, this guy yearns for the grand passion, for the female who awakens every cell of his being. His ideal girl is spiritual, creative, bold and beautiful, as amazed by the Universe as he is and just as much of an 'extreme-o-phile'. He's totally into true togetherness. Once in love, he wants to merge. Despising sycophants, he loves the woman who is first true to herself.

Ed Burns, Johnny Depp, Ralph Fiennes, Jude Law, Guy Ritchie, Will Smith

# Sagittarius

## November 23 - December 21

Cosmically activated by loud rock 'n' roll or
gratuitously 'free love' hippie music.
The Psyche-in-Saggo guy sees himself as a free
spirit who needs a sexy soundtrack.

He needs to know that she is untamable

The return of the lotus-eater; the man with Psyche in Saggo loves the woman who expands his horizons, blows his mind and then flits off unencumbered. His ideal girl is fun-loving, utterly uninhibited and able to relate to anyone. He is incapable of setting boundaries for the woman he loves — the louder and more vivacious she is the better. In his mind he wants to be in Shangri-la with his fun-loving adventure girl and someone who says about the impossible dream, 'Let's just do it!' She is completely candid — this man can't handle manipulators — and feels that she is as unlike 'the others' as he does.

Hugh Jackman, Ozzy Osbourne, Brad Pitt, Ian Somerhalder, Owen Wilson

# Capricorn

## December 22 - January 20

Cosmically activated by Top 40 soft rock. Not a
man who likes to be sidetracked, Mr Psyche in
Cap keeps to the musical straight and narrow.
If in doubt, check where his car radio is tuned.

He needs to know that the pursuit of success will
be mutual

This is the alpha guy in love. The dream girl of the guy with Psyche in Capricorn is a classic Type-A personality: vibrant, demanding and ambitious. He is most easily turned off by the victim stance or by a woman who wants to coast along on someone else's slog to success. His ideal female has poise, goals and a plan on which to structure her life. He likes the ones who don't need him. In fact, icy indifference inspires his ardour far more than over-the-top declarations of needy emotion. He fantasizes about being one part of a dynamic duo. These two are an unbeatable power couple.

Kieran Culkin, Ryan Phillippe

Soulmating

# Aquarius
## January 21 - February 19

Cosmically activated by German synthesizer
bands and symphonies played entirely with
drums. He has odd tastes in music: do your
homework before giving him a Céline Dion CD.

He needs to know that his mind
will be stimulated

Luckily, for some women, the man with Psyche in Aquarius is a connoisseur of female eccentricity. His ideal woman is a clear-thinking, way-ahead-of-her-time type of individual. A natural-born feminist sympathizer, he is not particularly keen on the usual 'tricks' of seduction and instead relishes the 'great minds thinking alike' paradigm. He likes it when a lover can challenge his preconceptions and turn him on to new ways of thinking about 'the obvious'. Though a romantic player when he wants to be, his soulmate must first access his mind and form a friendship.

Russell Crowe, Michael Douglas, Prince Harry

# Pisces

## February 20 - March 20

Cosmically activated by sexy, maybe even tarty
girl bands and female singers. He's openly
interested in sex and the idea of the sexy
chanteuse. Loves female musicians being
raunchy or naughty.

He needs to know that she is cuddly but difficult

Psyche in Pisces wants the impossible in a woman – an intriguing blend of vixenly cunning and baby-like innocence. His fantasy of the perfect woman is the most idealistic of all and can easily keep him from forming a real-life romance. His soulmate has to be someone fluid of personality, forever in flux, and yet also firm enough to keep a grip on herself amid the changing projections of Psyche in Pisces. Easily beguiled by beauty, he can also be at risk of falling in unrequited love. What better way to ensure that the excitement and allure he craves do not become overly real?

Luis Buñuel, Travis Fimmell

# Her Eros reveals.. her ideal man

'This relationship with David has taken
me totally by surprise, a wonderful surprise.
I have found my soulmate in him, my friend.
In him I have found my lover, my companion.
[He is] the person I was looking for — my other
half. I hope everyone in this world finds their
other half as I did mine.'

Uber-model Iman on her husband, rock star David Bowie

# Her Eros reveals ... her ideal man

**P**ut simply, a woman's Eros sign shows us the man she dreams about. Our masculine 'type' is so often formed fairly early in life, perhaps from a mish-mash of family and cultural influences — that childhood crush or (eek!) father figure.

But her Eros reveals the guy who can truly make her happy ... the one she needs as opposed to wants. Imagine a worldly and sophisticated Capricorn woman, predestined — she feels — for an official catch, a 'suit' if you like. But should her Eros be in bohemian Sagittarius, her real masculine ideal is more likely to turn up in surfer-dude guise.

It is vital that girls get to grips with their Eros sign as it represents the true lover. Only a man with at least some of the Eros 'cred' can totally ensnare her heart. The sign placement of Eros reveals how the woman's idealized lover figures above and beyond her more prosaic, real-life concerns.

The placement of Eros of actress Jennifer Aniston is exactly conjunct with the Eros of her husband, actor Brad Pitt. The same applies to actress Uma Thurman and her husband, actor Ethan Hawke. So the erotic ideals of these women are displayed by the choice of their men.

For ultimate happiness in love and to feel truly soulmated, the Eros sign must be able to find full expression along with the yearnings revealed by the sign placement of Psyche. The idea is to read both signs and gain more insight into what may be going on subconsciously, far beneath the so suave and sensible romantic persona du jour!

# Her Eros is in...

'I always had this dream of meeting an artist, an artist girl who would be like me. And I thought it was a myth, but then I met Yoko and that was it.'

Former Beatle John Lennon on his wife, artist Yoko Ono

'She is wild and innocent, pledged to love
Through all disaster; but those other women
Decry her for a witch or a common drab
And glare back when she greets them.
Here is her portrait, gazing sidelong at me,
The hair in disarray, the young eyes pleading:
"And, you, love? As unlike those other men
As I those other women?"'

*The Portrait* — Robert Graves

# Aries

## March 21 - April 20

Cosmically activated by the fire of a bloodstone.
Her fiery nature is triggered by firestones, rubies
and garnets. Burning red is forever her hue
du jour. She sizzles.

She wants to hear: I want you

Her dream lover? The wild-at-heart studly type whom only she seems capable of conquering. Up for a challenge, the Eros-in-Aries woman appreciates strength and success in men more than any other female. She likes to mess with the head of Mr Hard-To-Get, making him crash through new barriers of love and adoration. Far from upsetting her, healthy competition arouses her fighting instincts. It's vital that she feels superior to those who may have gone before. Once soulmated, her guy becomes the hero of her heart. Her loyalty is unsurpassed just as long as he first jumps through the hoops.

Pamela Anderson, Nicole Kidman, Madonna, Elle Macpherson

# Taurus

## April 21 - May 21

Cosmically activated by green from the Earth.
The Eros-in-Taurus girl is brought alive by
emerald, jade, greenstone, green tourmaline
and peridot. Think like her, think green.

She wants to hear: I'm here to stay

The woman with Eros in Taurus longs for a man who is the epitome of assurance and stability. She comes undone easily with jittery guys, tantrum-throwers and manipulators of girls. The man of her dreams must relish the non-stop slog to score his goals and feather their nest. Her fantasy is that of the insatiable sensualist at home and the dignified patriarch type everywhere else. She is naturally drawn to the mature, manly end of the male spectrum as opposed to the rowdy or uncertain iconoclast.

Britney Spears, Hilary Swank

# Gemini

## May 22 - June 21

Cosmically activated by pearls and pearls only.
The milky baubles are traditionally so-o-o lucky
for the Gemini woman, and for her only. Light
up the Eros-in-Gem girl with a special gift.

She wants to hear: I'm changeable,
very changeable

Eros in Gemini falls for the witty, silver-tongued guy. She loves the super-smart, mind-challenging man and is turned on by innuendo-laden gossip, over-the-top flirting and amazing new info. She's keen to try new things and will never allow dullness to darken her love life. Given this set of prerequisites, it is not surprising that the woman with Eros in Gemini is also known to crave variety in her menfolk. At some point it occurs to her that one man may not be able to satisfy her continual need for stimulation. The one who can is her soulmate.

Beyoncé Knowles, Mae West

# Cancer

## June 22 - July 23

Cosmically activated by moonstone, water sapphire, clear quartz crystal. Her favourite gemstones symbolize the power of pure clarity and illumination. She's a person of sensitivity — her stones must be as clear as her lover.

She wants to hear: I need a muse

It is almost impossible for the woman with Eros in Cancer to fall in love with a man who is not sensitive and creative. Men who are hardened to life, in an effort to fit in with the system, leave her cold. She idealizes the artist, the musician and the writer — the guy incapable of mortgaging his dreams for the sake of respectability. But, she is also very security conscious so her ideal soulmate is the one who somehow attains wealth by following his bliss. Highly intuitive and compassionate, her true lover is gentle and nurturing, never macho or blustering.

Drew Barrymore, Iman, Natalie Imbruglia, Courtney Love

# Leo

## July 24 - August 23

Cosmically activated by gold! The yellow metal is warm like the Sun and as precious as the Leo sense of self. Give the gift of gold and watch her fabulosity come to life.

She wants to hear: And you can be my queen!

Eros in Leo needs nothing less than a superstar of love. She is truly admiring of talent and success. Her ideal guy is a highly acclaimed limelight-hogger with a super ego, immense confidence and an extreme belief in himself. She always checks out the talent in a social situation, overlooking the less impressive man in favour of the most gorgeous and over-the-top stud. Her idea of love involves grandiose, never-ending romance and the luxurious life. She simply can't warm to someone who is insecure, shy or even vaguely undemonstrative.

Kirsten Dunst, Gwen Stefani,
Audrey Tautou, Catherine Zeta-Jones

# Virgo

## August 24 - September 23

Cosmically activated by lapis lazuli. Cool and
beautiful, just like the Eros-in-Virgo girl, the
ultramarine rock has associations as an
aphrodisiac and a health charm. Make her glow!

She wants to hear: I've already cleaned it

She likes the cute quirky guy who, closeted like Superman, turns into a very suave alpha male. Immune to braggart gesturing and shallow displays of affection, her heart is won by the insightful compliment, the truly thoughtful act of kindness. But her ideal man is above all witty and funny. Eros in Virgo falls in love with the brilliant raconteur, the guy who can make a hilarious morsel out of even the most banal detail of everyday life. She is not at all interested in the guys who alternate from wild flights of fancy to crashing insecurity. This woman appreciates sanity and urbanity.

Melanie Griffith, Angelina Jolie, Jada Pinkett Smith

# Libra

## September 24 - October 23

Cosmically activated by diamonds. When a woman has Eros in Libra, her heart yearns for harmony and enduring balance, on a highly sophisticated scale. The diamond she wears is aptly distinguished.

She wants to hear: I love you for your beauty

The girl just can't help it — she's a lover of male beauty in all its forms. And the man interested in hooking up with her has to acknowledge that she won't stop noticing the glory of masculine pulchritude just because she's soulmated. Eros in Libra adores not only good looks and charm but also the man of a philosophical bent, someone who can detach and consider both sides of an argument. Scenes and disharmony send her skittering away. An aesthetic creature at heart, she can't abide a man who makes scenes or who is bolshie and macho just for the sake of it.

Jade Jagger, Ashley Judd, Rachel Ward

# Scorpio

## October 24 - November 22

Cosmically activated by the dark stones. This woman's love nature is mysterious, which is not completely apparent on either the first or 10th meeting. Bring her the brooding malachite and black opal.

She wants to hear: You consume me

Eros in Scorpio doesn't even bother dating unless her knees tremble at the sheer sight of the guy. It's either intensely passionate or she's not there — literally. Her ideal man is super-focused on his brilliant career and his interests. One of his interests — her — could be better classified as an obsession. She is quickly bored with the guy who is too light-hearted about an affair and ditto the 'just good friends' dynamic. She already has plenty of friends, thank you. Her soulmate cares deeply about the world and is capable of being deeply moved by emotion.

Catherine Deneuve, Princess Diana, Charlize Theron

# Sagittarius
## November 23 - December 21

Cosmically activated by the blue-green rock.
As changeable as the Eros-in-Saggo girl herself,
turquoise is also about things that don't change,
such as love and loyalty.


She wants to hear: If it's the truth, it can't
be embarrassing

The woman with Eros in Saggo admires the independent man who makes up his own rules as he goes along. She also prefers the company of rugged idealists and bohemian dream boys. Her ideal man gives her stacks of space in which to develop by herself and hang out with her friends. A jealous or possessive male is like a bad nightmare. She needs someone secure in his own right to let her shine her own light in peace. Trust is her biggest motif in love and also the belief that 'truth is beauty'.

Christina Aguilera, Liv Tyler, Naomi Watts, Kate Winslet

# Capricorn
## December 22 - January 20

Cosmically activated by success without drama.
She craves status without gaudiness, which is
not always easy. The clean, successful statement
of silver and sapphire meets the brief.

She wants to hear: I'll look after this

Eros in Capricorn can't help but be drawn to the self-made man. A guy in charge of his destiny, the boss man, the rainmaker — all these are her archetypes of maleness. Luckily, she tends to scare off those she would consider dilettantes or wimps, leaving the field clear for her alpha-male ideal. Oddly enough, her preferences are often even more clearly delineated by early romantic experiences with immature men who bring only chaos and mess. This makes her even more certain that the love she craves must take place in a defined structure with rules.

Sarah Michelle Gellar, Jennifer Lopez,
Jennifer Love Hewitt, Kate Moss,
Brittany Murphy, Meg Ryan,
Danielle Spencer, Mena Suvari,
Uma Thurman

# Aquarius

## January 21 - February 19

Cosmically activated by amethyst, aka 'metamorphosis'. She is working at an elevated psychic level, so give her the rock that converts energies from low to high. Heavy stuff.

She wants to hear: This is about us, it's not about the rules

Her lover ideal is a rebel, nonconformist and politically progressive free spirit. She cares not for convention and often recoils from socially sanctioned lovers. Her dream is that she can have a relationship of equals, unmarred by fuddy-duddy ideas of what a love affair ought to be. The sexist or patronizing male does not stand a chance with this woman. Her heart is essentially free and the true lover of Eros in Aquarius is the man who wouldn't want to fence her in, even if he could. She's willing to wait for as long as it takes for that one guy who understands her on the spot.

Jennifer Aniston, Jennifer Connelly, Kate Hudson, Gwyneth Paltrow, Pink, Christy Turlington

# Pisces

## February 20 - March 20

Cosmically activated by a stone that enhances
her interest in the metaphysical. Eros in Pisces
is connected to other worlds, and aquamarine's
oceanic association is a great balancer.

She wants to hear: You have a temper?
I hadn't noticed

These girls are after Mr Unconditional Love. 'Do what thou wilt and I'll still adore you, darling' has to be the motto of he who would score her love. She is a frank admirer of men who are visionary, genius or artistic. Normality sends her shrieking off into the wilderness. Ditto what she considers to be petty judgments and silly expectations. Most of all, she wants to be with the guy who is truly compassionate. The harsh and cynical man is anathema to her tender soul. Naturally, the singer of love songs or the writer of beautiful poetry has a huge head start with her.

Victoria Beckham, Cameron Diaz, Missy Elliott, Elizabeth Hurley, Vanessa Paradis, Sarah Jessica Parker, Michelle Pfeiffer, Brooke Shields, Shania Twain, Reese Witherspoon

# Eros and Psyche in love - the soulmating maps

'I awake filled with thoughts of you. Your image and the intoxicating evening that we spent yesterday have left my senses in turmoil.Sweet, incomparable Josephine, what astrange effect you have on my heart.'

Emperor of France, Napoleon Bonaparte, in a letter to his wife, Josephine Beauharnais

'My dear Nora,
It has just struck me. I came in
at half past 11. Since then, I have
been sitting in an easy chair like
a fool. I could do nothing. I hear
nothing but your voice. I am like
a fool hearing you call me "Dear".'

Irish novelist James Joyce in a letter to his wife,

Nora Barnacle

# His Eros is in ...

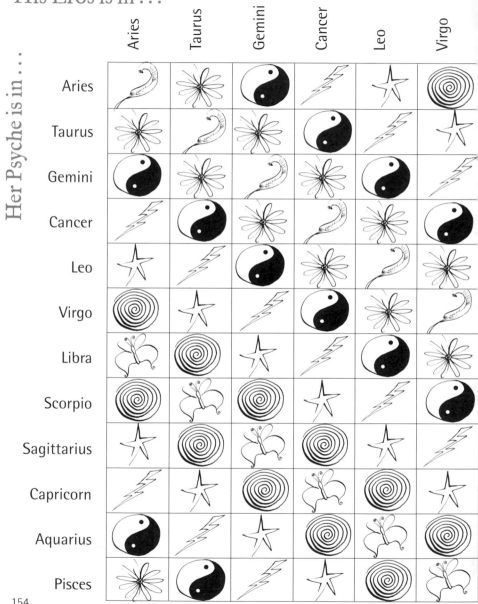

# Her Eros is in . . .

## His Psyche is in . . .

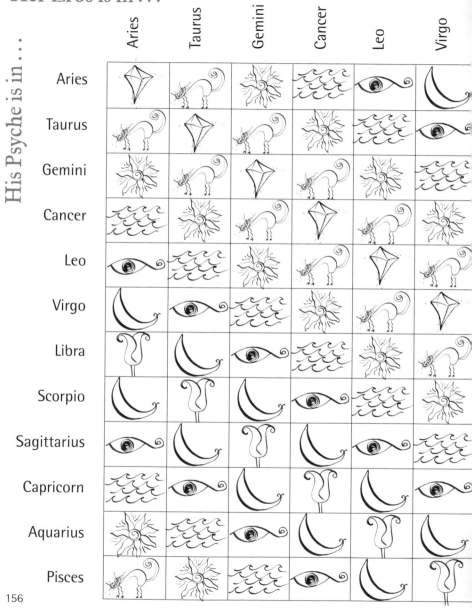

157

# His Eros - her Psyche

'It was like the old cliché where you see somebody, lock eyes across the room and time stands still.'

Actor Chad Lowe on meeting his wife, actress Hilary Swank at a party.

'We didn't date before we
married at all. We made *Bugsy*
together and, at the end of
the movie, I asked Annette if she
wanted to have dinner and have
a baby and she said yes. And we
did that night...'

Actor Warren Beatty on meeting his wife,
actress Annette Bening

# Feather

# Instantaneous combustion!

Wow! This is the classic love-at-first-sight scenario! So often it seems as though fate genuinely conspires to bring these two together under the most bizarre of circumstances. For example, she shouldn't have been there that night but she was and so she met him! When these two soulmates get together, each feels as though they are somehow coming home. It's similar to the sensation felt by a child, bored at a totally adult party, suddenly meeting another kid! No matter what the differences or even the geographical and cultural distance between them, they bond on the spot and forever at some level. Even if this duo meets but once, they will never forget one another and *that* encounter. And yet, this is the most likely relationship to go the distance, no matter what. Both people can't help but immediately sense the significance of the chemistry between them. They can run and they can hide but never deny the attraction.

Ryan Phillippe & Reese Witherspoon
Chris Henchy & Brooke Shields
Federico Fellini & Giuletta Masina
Liam Gallagher & Nicole Appleton
Ben Harper & Laura Dern

# Daisy

# The Weirding!

Ready or not, these two mess with one another's minds from the second they meet. They quite often start out with an official 'hate each other's guts' dynamic going on. They challenge each other to a strange 'who are you really?' duel of wits. Cosmically, they are destined to alter the other's reality to such an extent that, no matter what happens, life will never be quite the same again. Oddly enough, they tend to meet via normal circumstances. Perhaps they have even heard mention of the other for some time and vowed something like 'That person is so not me'! Yet, when they do meet up, they're irritated yet intrigued. Someone says one little thing and the other is like 'WHAT, did you say THAT?'. This liaison often lends itself to on-off-on-again shenanigans as each person must make huge adjustments to fit into the life path of the other — madly in love as they may be.

Richard Burton & Elizabeth Taylor
Guy Ritchie & Madonna
Russell Crowe & Danielle Spencer
Daniel Johns & Natalie Imbruglia

Soulmating

# Yin - Yang

# Collaborators in love

Serendipity strikes hard and fast as these two suddenly wake up to the fact that they're fully in love. Yes, this couple is the most likely to already know one another — perhaps they are even the clichéd 'just good friends', when suddenly one night, IT happens. Oh, dear. They're so naturally compatible and happy together that they often bond on a purely platonic level, knowing right from the start that this person is someone they want to have in their lives indefinitely. Consciously or otherwise, they don't want to blow it via some psychodramatic lust scenario. So? So they suppress their real feelings. Should true love run its destined course, this couple is a teamworking duo, evoking sustained mutual stimulation to help them ride out the ruts of long-term love. The best expression of this relationship is that of real partnering. They're mates in every sense of the word.

Bryan Brown & Rachel Ward
James Joyce & Nora Barnacle
David E Kelley & Michelle Pfeiffer
Graham Payn & Noël Coward

# Lightning Bolt

# Oh, God! I'm so in love!

Let's be quite clear about this one. It so often kicks off when one or both of the lovers are otherwise involved. Or, for some reason, the entire thing is utterly impossible. They meet, sense the heat and feel the fear. Each falls insanely in love and decides to ride it out like a kind of exotic flu. They frequently come across one another when every little thing goes against their romance. There is an initial encounter or two and then nothing. Yet something brings them back into contact with one another and it's all on – ready or not! Should they be wild enough to go ahead with this rollercoaster romance, they become the couple to watch. Each eggs on the other to fully follow their bliss. They take up all the oxygen in any room – the passion, the bitchery, the ego-conflicts. The sheer heat generated by this pair bonding is beyond belief.

Ethan Hawke & Uma Thurman
Johnny Depp & Vanessa Paradis
Antonio Banderas & Melanie Griffith
Sam Mendes & Kate Winslet
Michael Douglas & Catherine Zeta-Jones
Ed Burns & Christy Turlington
Ralph Fiennes & Francesca Annis
Matthew Broderick & Sarah Jessica Parker
Pete Sampras & Brigitte Wilson

Star

# Haven't we met before?

From the first moment they meet they're convinced that they know each other. And, in fact, this relationship is the most likely to begin with a massive confession session in which each feels compelled to tell ALL to the other. Afterward, neither can believe the inner *merde* they just told this person for no apparent reason. The soul link is profound and often signalled by a strong physical sensation. But it is not remotely lust-driven. It is, rather, a palpable shock of recognition – not the 'You ARE me' feeling generated by some of the other connections. It's a feeling of ease and luxury, like leaping into a hot opulent bath after battling through a long and stormy day of mundane crap. They feel understood as if for the first time and all of the ancient angst seems suddenly solved. This is one of the most likely 'together forever' soulmating scenarios.

Stephen Barlow & Joanna Lumley
Willie Gordon & Isabel Allende
Dario Franchitti & Ashley Judd
Will Smith & Jada Pinkett Smith
Oscar Wilde & Lord Alfred Douglas

# Butterfly

# Opposites attract but first repel!

Your friends suggest therapy as soon as possible but you don't give a damn what the shrink thinks. Nobody from the outside ever really gets this love affair but the people involved don't care. Not for one second. It is most likely to begin via an act of rebellion from one half of the pairing. Somehow, one of them is in riot about society and its expectations, so disillusioned and over love that it's not funny. This romance pops up as the proverbial bolt from the blue and each heals the other. It can even materialize like this: a brief encounter, a few words spoken and someone heads home to his or her life. The practical details of being together on a day-to-day basis bore this pair. They often seem to wind up in a dynamic that encourages them to polarize like a long-distance romance or some reason why they can't be too involved with one another's family. That's how it goes. And, as you might expect, this is an attraction that can quickly blow over. But, when it doesn't? It lasts forever and a day. And still nobody understands.

Freddie Prinze Jr & Sarah Michelle Gellar
Spencer Tracy & Katharine Hepburn
Bernard-Henri Levy & Arielle Dombasle
Jack London & Charmian Kittredge
Kid Rock & Pamela Anderson

Spiral

# Married already!

Hello, you must be my husband! Wife? Whatever, this duo knows quick smart that they're on, or off. They either get it on from the start or neatly avoid one another. Another way of putting it is that there is either no chemistry whatsoever between them or it is on from the literal second they see each other. If it's an on situation, they are so prone to skipping the usual courtship stage that it's ludicrous. People can't believe that these lovers haven't known one another since childhood! They often even look similar! They are the couple most likely to nauseate others via an extreme public intimacy dynamic. Speech, gags and even sexual preferences seem like suddenly shared secrets. If one, the other or both are accustomed to full-on tension between lovers, this relationship will freak them out at first. The comfort zoning is immense. Warning: even if these two do break up, they never truly split up, you understand.

David Beckham & Victoria Beckham
Ben Lee & Claire Danes
Royston Langdon & Liv Tyler
Danny DeVito & Rhea Perlman
Ben Stiller & Christine Taylor
Tim McGraw & Faith Hill

# Her Eros - his Psyche

'But we had talked for 10 hours without noticing the time passing. I let myself into my apartment thinking elatedly, "I have met the man I want to marry."' Gone were doubts about the existence of real love. I wasn't anywhere near understanding it yet, but I was full of joy.'

US novelist Madeleine L'Engle on meeting her husband, actor Hugh Franklin

Rochester: 'I knew you would do
me good in some way, at some
time: I saw it in your eyes
when I first beheld you; their
expression and smile did not ...
strike delight to my very inmost
heart so for nothing...'
Jane: 'I had not intended to
love him; the reader knows I had
wrought hard to extirpate from
my soul the germs of love there
detected; and now, at the first
renewed view of him, they
spontaneously revived, great
and strong! He made me love
him without looking at me ...
Reader, I married him.'

*Jane Eyre* — Charlotte Brontë

# Diamond

# Immortal lovers

A single mad moment often defines this love affair, probably the one with the highest soulmating potential of all! The second these two encounter each other, there is no room for anyone else. Memories of past lovers flee from their suddenly addled minds. They realize immediately that nothing, no matter what the complications, is going to stand between them and their goal to fulfil this liaison. One of the most surreal aspects of the diamond relationship is that one or both of the 'adorees' will have dreamt of it beforehand, perhaps even repeatedly. So it feels like it is the most deja vu thing ever. There is often some sort of sign or significant something worn or uttered in the initial meeting and neither will ever forget this conversation. Ready or not, they meet and realize that (eeek!) this is likely to be one of the most significant romances of their lifetime! Another cosmic clue: they are destined to deeply inspire one another creatively.

Edna St Vincent Millay & Eugene Boissevain
Helena Christensen & Norman Reedus
Laura Dern & Ben Harper

Cat

# Mind mates!

These two enjoy a love affair that gets better and better with time. Gossipy intimacy and shared dreams bring them closer together. Upon first meeting one another, they feel — if not a striking moment of lust — a strong sensation of friendship. It's like the trust and familiarity of good mates is with them right from the start. There seems little need to explain much to each other. This is also the couple most likely to succeed together. They totally 'get' one another's mindset and let nothing erode their mutual loyalty. In fact, it is often work or business of some sort that brings them together at first. They weave around them a tight little web of friends and family, ensuring that their own romancing does not inhibit a broader social push. Together they are easily more than the sum of their parts. Astro ick factor: they could wind up vibing more like close siblings than lovers.

Rachel Ward & Bryan Brown
Danielle Spencer & Russell Crowe
Sharon & Ozzy Osbourne
Ashley Judd & Dario Franchitti

Sun

# Deja vu!

Love comes quickly as neither party in this magical pair-bonding can believe their luck. They are often introduced by mutual friends who seem to sense their extreme compatibility well before the Sun couple gets it. Somehow, a bizarre factor seems to come between these two at first — there is always a challenge to overcome. Perhaps the strong presence of an ex-lover? Domineering or disapproving family? Total fear of succumbing to the passion? Whatever it may be, the couple either race off in different directions (yet never quite forgetting the feelings evoked by the other) or become much closer by joining to dissolve the love obstacle. Get between these two at your own peril. More than any other type of couple, they deeply admire one another and will do whatever it takes to protect their romance from toxic emotions or outside interference.

Brad Pitt & Jennifer Aniston
Iman & David Bowie
Kirsten Dunst & Jake Gyllenhaal
Naomi Watts & Heath Ledger
Gwen Stefani & Gavin Rossdale
Danny DeVito & Rhea Perlman
Christine Taylor & Ben Stiller
Jada Pinkett Smith & Will Smith

# Waves

# Karma drama!

These two are totally destined to meet and make a maximum impact upon one another. This cosmic scenario naturally makes for some tempestuous scenes along with the classic make up/ break up dynamic. Just as waves allow the ocean to craft a relentless change to a coastline, the Waves relationship is about long-term transformations. These soulmates often have to face challenges to be with their lover and then the affair becomes its own pressure cooker of change. It's as if, despite their deep and abiding attraction toward one another, neither can be in the relationship as they are. The romance thus proves cathartic with each party ringing in profound changes: personality, beliefs, goals, lifestyle — even looks. The most instant manifestation of this so-destined love affair is that each person seems to begin a process of metamorphosis. Some call it crazy love but this destined duo doesn't give a damn.

Elizabeth Taylor & Richard Burton
Melanie Griffith & Antonio Banderas
Denise Richards & Charlie Sheen
Elin Nordegren & Tiger Woods
Christy Turlington & Ed Burns
Sarah Jessica Parker & Matthew Broderick
Brigitte Wilson & Pete Sampras
Faith Hill & Tim McGraw

# Eye

# You are my everything!

This tender romance has the potential to be the clingiest of all! Once pair-bonded, this couple can be almost inseparable. They literally find being parted from one another to be *that* irksome. Some have love at first sight, others get a bolt from the blue; peace relationships are often built on emotional and social togetherness before any passion sneaks in. This doesn't mean there isn't any excitement — it just means the tension builds to the heat of that first kiss. These guys know each other by the way each feels serene and kind of blissed out by the whole thing. Life itself seems to conspire to bring them together. It's as if they can see all the 'fragile , handle with care' areas of other relationships and not only tread around them but actually heal the psychic scars from any ancient angst.

Vanessa Paradis & Johnny Depp
Fanny Ardant & François Truffaut
Reese Witherspoon & Ryan Phillippe
Amelia Earhart & George Palmer Putnam
Jennifer Lopez & Ben Affleck
Natalie Portman & Gael Garcia Bernal
Francesca Annis & Ralph Fiennes

# Moon

# Always on my mind!

Always evolving, this relationship is perpetual poetry in motion and a non-stop work in progress. It is as if each 'adoree' must make constant — if tiny — attitude adjustments in order to let the love affair shine. If one or the other gets too stuck in a certain paradigm, the whole liaison starts to stall and, if they are not careful, bog down. It is amazing how often this romance is characterized by one of the parties loathing (or at least not much liking!) the other person. Yet, if this is the case, there will nonetheless be a kind of incessant buzz at the back of their mind. Once sighted, these guys are never out of one another's minds. Another astro clue: they often meet each other at a time of personal crisis. The mutual emotion is like 'Whoah! And now this!' They are also highly likely to be a 'rebound' affair — albeit one that may go on forever!

Uma Thurman & Ethan Hawke
Kate Hudson & Chris Robinson
Gwyneth Paltrow & Chris Martin
Charmian Kittredge & Jack London
Natalie Imbruglia & Daniel Johns

# Tulip

# We may never come this way again!

The dynamic tension generated by this pairing is truly something to behold. Often they are officially the complete opposite of one another. No? Something is bound to be diametrically opposed. They get it on via an instant emotion of not 'Wow, we are so similar' but of 'You complete me'. Happier than any other kind of couple to not just tolerate but relish the differences between them, they give one another 'free to be me' room. They're also suave, modern and worldly about gender expression, caring not about who seems to be 'in charge'. Deeply private and always discreet, they keep the real passion and power politics to themselves, to be played out in private. This is because, cosmically, this duo always has something hot to be, er, worked through.

Hilary Swank & Chad Lowe
Yoko Ono & John Lennon
Kate Winslet and Sam Mendes,
Madeleine L'Engle and Hugh Franklin
Candice Bergen & Louis Malle

.

# How your Sun sign gets it on with Eros & Psyche

# If you are an Aries...
## March 21 to April 20

You are a self-actualizing and upbeat egomaniac. Nobody tells you what to do or how to do it. Over the top? For sure. As ultra-Aries fashionista diva Diana Vreeland said, 'exaggeration is the only reality.' You believe — along with (brilliant painter, sculptor, architect, engineer, musician etc) Leonardo da Vinci — that 'every object yields to stern resolve.' You're hyper-competitive in love, needing both a full-on challenge and non-stop drooling adulation. Hard to get? You bet. Difficult? You're officially impossible. You can be so prone to seeing even a much-adored lover as a mere blip on the radar of your genius. But whoever wins your love will be assured of an almost insanely loyal life partner.

# and your Eros is in...

# Soulmating

### ARIES

Okay, so you're an Aries by nature and an Aries in love! The good news is that there is no conflict between your core persona and the character you become when smitten. But, wow! Are you aware of how mega-demanding you can be? You ideally take steps to ameliorate bolshie tendencies. Admitting the occasional vulnerability does not render you a gimp. You can also be impatient with other people's displays of 'weakness'. To do ASAP: Learn the art of graceful apology and how to at least fake sympathy. Say 'sweetie.'

### TAURUS

Own up! You are secretly turned on by displays of status and/or economic prowess. You notice those luxury cars. But, yes, you come across as a hell of a lot more dependable than the average Sun sign Aries. You're also more in touch with your physical self and sensual needs. Aries says 'You want me or not? Because if you don't, there's plenty who do!'You apply clichéd seduction techniques. And you know they work!

Astro speciality: You love mood music, especially those cool DIY compilations. You are the DJ of love.

### GEMINI

The Aries part of you is direct. But Eros in Gemini makes you relish the art of mind-gaming. Aries is morality driven and *très* harsh on those deemed to be sleazy. Eros in Gemini is incapable of judgment, especially about anything to do with love, lust or soulmating. So your love life is about constantly reconciling the contradictions that make you so cute. Vow now: forgive and forget yourself. Love thyself as a so-complex creature, forever in flux and loving it!

Your astro alibi: Mild mendacity retains your mystique.

## CANCER

Aries doesn't give a damn about security. Your Aries Sun part of you is willing to throw everything away on a 'Respect me or else!' whim or to fulfil a feral crush that hit five minutes ago. Your Cancerian Eros craves comfort zoning and continuity of experience. What to do? Accept that when it comes to romance, you are a far clingier creature than the 'average' Aries. You are also kinder and more emotionally intelligent.

Astro witchery: Create the cosiest boudoir in the world. Satisfy that Aries ego by thinking 'pouncing pit'.

## LEO

Who can hack the heat of your radiant charisma! Eros in Leo adds feline grace to your Aries Sun schtick. You're a natural-born show-off diva, the performance artiste of love. So what alienates wannabe lovers? Grandiose vanity? Insatiable ego? Hmm. Yet you are also glamorous, inspirational and giving of yourself. Don't deny dramatic tendencies. Exaggerate!

Cosmic love tips: Learn several romantic poems off by heart for reciting to rapt potential adorees. Candlelight is your at-home equivalent of airbrushing.

## VIRGO

'Don't bug me with details,' barks Aries, whirling off in a haze of bliss-following genius. But Eros in Virgo does bother about the details, especially with relationships. You fall instantly in love, start 'creatively visualizing' the romance and then, before anything has even happened, you panic about where the two of you are going to live or indulge a 'what if the in-laws hate me?' fantasy.

Celestial mission: Please don't undermine your sexy and suave wordly love style via low-rent neurosis. What's it to be — crow's feet or laughter lines?

# Soulmating

### LIBRA

As an Aries, you can make up your mind about anything in two minutes flat. Quick and decisive, you're a legend. Or are you? Eros in Libra likes the multi-view. The Aries you despairs at this dithering but it helps make you human! You can deal with romantic ambiguity. You score big time in the dishing-out-(good-) advice stakes. You are the confidante, not the dictator, of love.

Astro bonus: You are far more sophisticated than 'normal' Arians. Just don't tell them. But you can't wait to find one and boast! See? You are an Aries.

### SCORPIO

Who cares what the shrink thinks? Not you. With the Sun in Aries and Eros in Scorpio, you're a free-wheeling individualista. You've got the gung-ho gorm of Aries blended with Scorp inscrutability. Ideally, Aries, positivity and self-belief enlighten the sometimes melancholy Scorp persona. Then, let the Scorpy depth of perception inform the oft-shallow Aries' world view! Voila! Meaningful and deep Aries spunk with attitude.

Scary astro fact: You're too busy ranting on to notice how seductive you are. Mirror, mirror?

### SAGITTARIUS

Sweet candour? Or bloody minded tactlessness? As both Aries and Sagittarius place high value on honesty, you find it almost impossible to deceive. This works for and against you. Yes, people trust you. And no matter what your chronological age, you come across as forever young and breezy. No, they don't necessarily enjoy hearing your unpolished version of reality.

Cosmic lesson du jour: Truth is not necessarily beauty — well, certainly not in a relationship. Finessing a compliment is not an ethical betrayal of principles.

## CAPRICORN

You're a seductive force to behold. Eros in Capricorn gives a grown-up, sophisticated kind of allure. Your Sun in Aries can dazzle anyone. But Aries is the baby of the Zodiac and Capricorn the know-all ancient. These influences can work at odds against one another. For example, you vibe arch old fogie when a breathless 'Oh, golly!' would work wonders. But, then you come off sounding anarchic and callow in a chat about income tax brackets. Reverse that paradigm and pull!

Cosmic sex flash: Love on the job is always an issue.

## AQUARIUS

As an Aries, you're simple and demonstrative in love. However, Eros in Aquarius complicates the scenario. An aspect of you is practically robotic, able to grasp romance in theory but not wanting to 'lower' yourself. Intimacy issues? 'I love you' says Mr/Ms Maybe. You change the subject to some article on human cloning law you read.

Astro romance resolution: You know all those meaningless bourgeois gestures? Flowers? Extravagant compliments? Moonlight declarations of intent? Love song requests? Just do them.

## PISCES

You are both the macho warrior king or queen and the prince or princess bride. Thing One and Thing Two? Aries is ultra-assertive and strident. Eros in Pisces operates on a subliminal level, intuiting realities way below the radar of optimistic but brash Aries. People go ape for this combo of confidence and modesty. How do you pull it off? You have no idea. But you're at your best au naturel — hideous when contrived.

Cosmic memo: Retain your idealism. Try not to ring your ex-(or future) lovers for moral support during a date.

# Or your Psyche is in...

### ARIES

Do you have sky-high expectations in love? Inner you and outer you are a perfect match! Blessed with a strong sense of self-worth, you are also prone to sudden insecurity crashes. How to reboot? You need flattery and stacks of it. Your motto: life's too short to be subtle. But do bear in mind that with this placement comes rabid antagonism. You're also argumentative.

Astro flash: MAD (Mutually Assured Destruction) is a geopolitical concept, not a romantic policy. Got it?

### TAURUS

As an Aries, you're often hyper-boho. Screw convention. The only system you're interested in is your own Aries-archy. But Psyche in Taurus counteracts that gung-ho attitude. You like things to be done right. You need relationships to follow a prescribed path. People who don't appreciate your boundaries are quickly ousted.

What to do: Eschew tacky scenarios. Casual sex creates casual enemies. Accept your 'inner straight'.

### GEMINI

You're flash, swank and fickle, the playgirl/playboy of love. If someone's easy on the eye, you'll wink. You say whatever it takes to make the point du jour. People are so confounded by the complexity beneath your cultivated air of simplicity. Aries keeps no secrets — why bother? Psyche in Gemini has stacks. For inner peace you need privacy of mind, that 'something stupid' go-nowhere flirtation, the frisson with someone so off limits.

Cosmic love task: Re-read the fable about the goose and the gander.

## CANCER

Aries is anti-nostalgia. Officially, you abhor sentiment. Everyone knows that you live in the now. So, how do you justify your Cancerian Psyche? The part of you that reveres the past, tradition and sentimental keepsakes? No way are you going to shred those erotic love notes from yesteryear! You're torn between getting on with it and wallowing in ancient angst from some long-gone, doomed-before-it-even-began excuse for a love affair.

Hot astro hint: Always re-route that clandestine slushy emotion into the current love reality.

## LEO

You are a 'no frills' simple soul. The psycho-theatrics of love do not intrigue you. Like hell they don't! Eros in Leo equips you for the most lavish production of all — the pure weight of your heart — and its diva demands. Aries and you screech on about honesty. Psyche in Leo likes the mega-scene. Your entrance makes the paparazzi go wild. All eyes are upon you. Even when you're technically losing it in sensual ecstasy.

Karma drama: The spectre of the Elizabeth Taylor/Richard Burton superstar relationship.

## VIRGO

Bolshie Ballet? Psyche in Virgo makes Aries and you fantasize about perfect poise. You guilt yourself for saying the wrong thing, not saying anything. In an extreme self-guilting orgy you're angry at yourself for just being: let your Aries Sun reassure Psyche in Virgo over-analysis. Yet it is also this Psyche of yours that bestows supernatural self-assurance and observational skills beyond the ken of the 'average' Aries.

Cosmic love cure: Seek a second opinion for self-diagnosed personality deficits. Judge not lest you know this one!

# Soulmating

### LIBRA

You can go it alone anytime. It's a point of major pride, your core competency and complete crap. With Psyche in Libra, you seek love's paradise. Suave as always, you go along with the general hoo-hah but your heart yearns for life lived in tandem with a truly significant other. Pretend your pretty head off but please don't undermine yourself by mixing with people who disrespect you and your not-so-secret true romance agenda.

Cosmic love mission: To avoid mixed messaging. Tame the ego ASAP. Be open to all options.

### SCORPIO

The Aries you is like the nightclub of love. You're raunchy, ready to get it on and damn the consequences. But, beyond the 'shiny disco balls, late-night calls' reality, the tide of your heart is always high. Admit it. You're a romantic. Psyche in Scorpio runs so deep that you're constantly tweaking different acts — Brave New Aries and Scorp of Mystery.

Astro flash: Stop alternating between being brash in situations of bona-fide intimacy and hyper-intense when it's not appropriate. Naivete is so non-you. The one you love arrives quietly.

### SAGITTARIUS

The performance-driven Aries You wants to score at all costs, whether it be for a minute or a lifetime. It's all about Brand You and ego on the sleeve — where is the heart? Your Psyche in Sagittarius is light-in-love, able to seize the passing joy without seeking to conquer. You'll dutifully shoulder the factory worker 'burden' of everyday relationship whilst cherishing the blissful fantasy of some fleeting attraction.

Astro love karma: To merge your romantic-escape artiste dream with an actual real-life romance. Flirt! Even as you do your tax together!

## CAPRICORN

'Do what thou wilt' — you want the one you love to be happy, no matter what it takes. Non-profit yoga someplace daggy? Hmm. Maybe not. Psyche in Capricorn kicks in and so it should! Worldly, wise and wealthy is the comfort zone of your soul. Your true love is as ambitious and on-message as you. Relaxation doesn't relax you. Only accomplishment creates the serenity you dream about. You and your soulmate scheme in harmony.

Astro nightmare to avoid: Needing a note from his/her accountant before you date.

## AQUARIUS

In love you are your partner's biggest fan ever. You're utterly supportive in every respect. Except one. Sucky flattery. You love to receive it and, in fact, contrive matters to ensure that your ego is lavishly serviced twice hourly. In public, you're adoring and doting spouse-ish. Behind the scenes, you pull major 'Don't you know who I am?' stunts, then quickly retiring to your 'den' whenever the conversation gets too real.

Cosmic love lesson: To grasp the idea that you — lovely *you*! — may actually be emotionally dependent upon another.

## PISCES

You're so straightforward, you take no crap — what you see is what you get. Or is it? Beneath that flashy Aries exterior lurks Psyche in Pisces, the most idealistic and toxically flirtatious of all! Yes, you. Own up! You love to be the off-limits object of desire almost as much as you yearn to be faithfully, slavishly adored. Whenever your love life weirds out, just know that it's you being surreal — yet again.

Astro karma: To own your own magic, to be psychically faithful and to meet someone just like You. Fresh linen rebirths you.

# If you are a Taurus...
## April 21 to May 21

You're ruled by Love Goddess Venus and an official cutie-pie but, à la actress Penélope Cruz, you're 'more tough than sweet'. Yes, along with Goddess-given allure comes a hefty dose of grit. You're a long-haul success machine, always willing to put in the extra slog to secure your aims in life. You're dependable, physically and mentally robust, but so stubborn that your personality can verge on tyrannical. You are perhaps the ultimate marital catch. Few other Sun signs can match your combo of sensuality, devotion and dedication to life goals.

The ick factor: You can become stuck, overly obstinate and quite fearful of change. As Hollywood hunk George Clooney says, 'Trying not to be a dick takes work'.

# and your Eros is in...

## ARIES

You think you're so straight but you're really a flake! At least, you are the second your heart gets engaged. The Taurean You believes in The Rules. Eros in Aries says 'stuff the rules — let's go there!' and you do. You'll throw over yonks of sensible achievement (maybe even a logical but non-fulfilling relationship) to pursue someone you met just once. Taurus values steadiness. Eros in Aries wants the zing! This so freaks you out.

Astro destiny: Long-term supportive and sensible love affair plus sexual bliss and excitement ... who? Dreams tell all.

## TAURUS

Both your Sun and Eros are ruled by Venus. Your luscious gorgeousness and radiantly long-term loyalty potential reels in would-be lovers like no other earthly creature. You say 'hello' and they hear 'I love you'. You spend a lot of time quelling misconceptions about your availability. In your mind, you run forever free in some grassy pasture, holding out for the ultimate. It happens the second you get over yourself.

Celestial love lesson: The soulmate is (apparently) immune to your beauty ... you bond mentally.

## GEMINI

The Taurean You seeks civilized stability, the no-explanations-needed, relax-at-last comfort zone of home. But the Eros-in-Gemini You enjoys destabilizing anything that's settled. Not that you will admit to this dynamic. So, if you're home in your zone and exchange glances with the cute tradesman, the Taurean You will guilt out for days. However, Eros in Gemini *milks* it for fun and extra-teasing potential within the core love relationship.

Astro karma drama: You go for the Suit archetype but, really, you need a silver-tongued split persona à la secret you!

## CANCER

Taurus says 'just give me the facts' — the Cancerian Eros wants to know 'how did you feel?' You can't fancy anyone without getting a huge blast of where they are at emotionally. It's concurrently your liability and asset. You see behind the props of macho bluster or that awkward bombshell pose. It's a blessing for true love and friendship, an immediate sop upon any form of casual flirtation.

Cosmic love lessons: Do not waste your pearls of wisdom on swines who just don't get it. Do not phone every half hour just to check that they still love you.

## LEO

As a Taurus, you are the most adequate sign of all. A dependable force for stability, you don't like to make 'a fuss' about anything. But your Eros in Leo demands fuss. That scene? Flared nostrils, raised perfect brows and beautiful hair? That was not the Taurean You. It was luvvie Leo, demanding proper attention. In love, you need to seduce like a Leo and that means a little drama. No way will you be overlooked for even a moment.

Celestial solar hotness memo: Beautiful hair sets the scene. The moment is all. Vanity *is* Zen.

## VIRGO

One burp and it's all off! This happens the moment you fall in love, lust or when your Eros in Virgo steps in, just to make sure that your Taurus self is not too trusting. Taurean You vibes off physical impressions (scent? gorgeousness quotient? body tone?) but your Virgoan Eros seeks sanity, decency and productive function in society. No matter how mysterious or joyful the encounter, Eros in Virgo is there as the police officer. Yes, this can be a barrier between you and love.

Astro memo: Think discrimination – not random nitpickery.

## LIBRA

You're criminally cute and, worse, cosmically hard-wired to run several lovers at once. Yes, of course you can settle down with just one but he or she would have to be extremely, er, multifacteted. The Taurus You is uni-minded and definite. Eros in Libra finds serenity by never making up his or her mind ... for sure. The path of pleasure and fun lies in remaining always open to possibilities or another point of view.

Celestial love lesson: To accept that your love life is supposed to be a mental expansion trip for you!

## SCORPIO

What's weird about your love life? There's drama-disdaining You, so correct and proper that you verge on pod-personage. Then there's your sensation-seeking Eros in Scorpio.

What to do: Ideally, accept that you require a certain degree of intensity and mystique in romance. Deny this longing and it blows back at you in the form of high mega-maintenance lovers. That's right. If you're dating a string of crypto-hysterical nympho compulsives, you are, in fact, attracting repressed aspects of yourself! Don't deconstruct *them*! You?

## SAGITTARIUS

Being a Taurus is about certainty. But Eros in Sagittarius is a wanderlusting free spirit. Someplace in your mind is a secret island where attractive and undemanding natives worship you as God or Goddess. But, you also want Mr or Mrs Reliable, someone who actually gets off on your anal control-freaky to-do lists and endless crusading recommendations re food, dining room furniture, fingernails ... whatever. Get a grip?

Good romance karma: Non-vocational 'just because' courses of study, especially if exotic travel is involved.

## CAPRICORN

The good news is that Taurus (your Sun sign) and Capricorn (your Eros sign) are both Earth signs and thus extremely compatible. You have little conflict between your core persona and getting-it-on character. You're strong, sexy and hideously ambitious. Success is a huge turn-on for you along with people who are physically toned and together.

The astro weirding: You can have this compulsion to shack up with someone completely unlike you and then turn him or her into a *clone of you* via corrective nagging. Ugly.

## AQUARIUS

The Taurean You is a sensual beast, renowned for insatiable libido and hardcore money-grubbing. You'll do whatever it takes to feather a secure little nest for you and yours. But Eros in Aquarius switches off sexually when in love! Yes, this can translate into a rather tedious Madonna-Whore/Prince-Bastard complex. You're unintentionally cruel, the benevolent dictator of love.

Cosmic task: Realize that lust at first sight rarely works out for you. The friendship must be allowed to form first. Hint: But don't hit on friends unless your intentions are pure.

## PISCES

This cute little astro combo makes you captivating beyond reason. You are poetry in motion. Or, okay — because this is Taurus, after all — poetry slacking off on the couch. The joy of being a Taurus with Eros in Psyche is that you come across like some wild romantic, convinced that every object of your lust is the reincarnation of a past life lover (you gotta watch this!). Then, but when things get real, you are fully present, sensual and aware! You are the magical realist of love.

Astro nightmare: Dutifully sticking with someone who's inferior.

# Or your Psyche is in...

## ARIES

You claim to crave the peaceful life but really you're just after a good scrap! No, this does not have to be a dysfunctional dynamic. Think more that apart from the usual Taurean life mission (a comfy castle with adoring family, respectable position in society, et al) you've got an internal quest going on. You're a person of purity and such lightness can attract muddier types in early love life. You may find heart's ease via the not-so-scenic gutter detour. Astro flash: Your soulmate is adoring but takes no crap.

## TAURUS

Taurus You and your Soul sign (Psyche in Taurus) are in sweet agreement. The way you project is how you are! Your Taurean Psyche values loyalty above all else. You are a moral person, capable of cutting off another person forever, should they not live up to your ethical code. This, while admirable, can create difficulties. Astro lesson: To not miss out on following your bliss by being overly judgmental — that is, you're a thundering bore mid-rant.

## GEMINI

Congratulations! This is one of the Sun sign-Psyche sign combos most likely to drive lovers utterly bats! Not that you'd notice. You're a blend of 'go hard or go home' material demands — your ideal person is successful or else — and a secretly quixotic, fickle little heart. It's like you get a banker partner and then use some of the money to fund your secret anarchist lover. That's an extreme example but, admit it! You don't *want* to be understood! Celestial hint: Weave variety into the structure of la vie en Cow.

# Soulmating

## CANCER

Okay, so you're a hoarder and maybe your house does remind people of an ill-curated museum but you have the potential to be such a holistically together person! Just keep on talking to yourself. Not in the mad-mutterings-on-street sense but via attunement to real emotions. Taurus is prone to taking things on face value. Your Psyche sign is clairvoyant: you intuit people's hidden motivations. Access your inner druid/druidess dude!

Cosmic love secret: Your ideal lover relates to the spiritual you as well as the rest of you.

## LEO

The Taurean You may be super-sensible but your Psyche in Leo is not! Taurus can say 'Yes!' to a less-than-thrilling relationship paradigm, perhaps even to keep (eeek!) the peace. You can get stuck in a tedious scenario, just because it's familiar. But your Psyche sign needs to be worshipped! You will never be truly content in a lukewarm love affair ... Happiness lies in honouring your Leonine Psyche's desire for glamour and beauty.

Stellar spell: Believe it or not, beautiful hair is the beginning of unfurling your Leo self.

## VIRGO

Taurus is one of the most sensual signs of all and Psyche in Virgo is a successful seducer/seductress by dint of being able to zoom in on another's every personality foible. So, you're so suave in love. But the 'curse' of Psyche in Virgo is that penchant for self-guilting. You judge yourself by standards you would never dream of applying to friends et al, let alone the lovers who swarm around you. It's true. Would you say to a friend who's freshly fallen in love: 'What if you undress and he hates your thighs?'

Cosmic coupling: First love thyself.

# LIBRA

Love me for whoever I am, dammit! One moment you want your hard slog and professionalism to be admired. Then, the next moment, you're whining about being adored in spite of it. The Taurus You finds a centre and stays there. Some would say that you get *stuck* there. Psyche in Libra needs to alter his/her position several times a day. It bugs you? Imagine how it affects lovers. But, guess what? It's you. And, by trying to become too fixed, you lose something precious.

Astro flash: You're Yin-Yang, Yang-Yin, Yang-Yang, Yin...

# SCORPIO

There you are, trying to get it on with Mr/Mrs Suitable when someone so freaky but gorgeous seemingly dives into your life. It's going to keep on happening! Your Psyche in Scorpio wants more than Sun in Taurus. You want more heat, passion and mystery. More, *more*. To honour your Scorpy Psyche, try tarot card reading, kung fu, super-modelling, deep-sea diving, advocacy work for victims of sex abuse, bodybuilding.

Cosmic love lesson: You will never be satisfied with a merely convenient liaison. It's soulmating or nothing!

# SAGITTARIUS

Taurus is the most settled Sun Sign of all. Psyche in Sagittarius is restless — mentally, emotionally and, yes (!), physically. Go too much with the Taurus aspect of yourself and you risk becoming stultified, prematurely aged and prone to random bitchery. No matter how much in love you are, your spiritual wellbeing relies upon frequent escapes to the wilderness, thought leadership and/or just the simple scoring of solo Q-time.

Astro hint: Acknowledging your independence flushes out the true pair-bonding that you need.

## CAPRICORN

Your Sun Sign (Taurus) and your Psyche Sign of Capricorn are ultra-compatible. Your core persona and your soul are admirably in sync. Success in every area is, you feel, your birthright. And, you're so right! You tend to attract partners who can and will make you happy! And your discriminatory powers are so honed that you rarely waste precious time and energy on non-you lovers. Possible ick factor: To be orgasmic or else. You're mega-sensual. Like it or not, sexual compatibility must be paramount for long-term satisfaction in a relationship.

## AQUARIUS

Taurus is a huge fan of the status quo. Aquarius seemingly exists to stuff around with it. You're both! What to do? Some people with this fascinating combo act it out by becoming, say, a corporate lawyer who dates an anti-globalization activist. But, deep down, you know that the solution lies in being both yourself: you somehow need to fulfil your yearnings for comfort and respectability whilst also letting radical you express him/herself. Astro flash: Your ideal lover is a BoBo (Bourgeois-Bohemian), just like you! You're so modern.

## PISCES

The secret of being a Taurus with Psyche in Pisces? Not going too far into either paradigm. You need to be free but within boundaries. Your Taurus side flourishes via routine and money! The Pisces You rebels against societal demands. It's the part of you that wants to stay up all night wearing retro-lingerie or polka-dot pajamas, scribbling poetry, throwing the I-Ching and contemplating the crush du jour. Taurus needs to get up at 6am to make the gym before work. You send people absolutely gaga with this kind of behaviour. Lucky you're so alluring.

# If you are a Gemini...

## May 21 to June 21

There's two of you! Yes, you're born under the sign of the Twins. So Twin One is blithe, amusing and always informed. Twin Two is a heartless and amoral flake. Light-hearted, easily bored and seemingly able to process any emotion whatsoever in five minutes flat, you're the heartbreaker of the Zodiac. Some call you fickle but you go along with the Chinese sage Confucius (another Gemini) that 'only the wisest and the stupidest never change'. Irked as you can be by the demands of everyday love, you can be up for the unrequited romance or secret frisson that is never quite kept at an exciting boil.

# and your Eros is in...

# Soulmating

### ARIES

It's you! You're the person people grizzle to advice columns about. You come on strong and then, wham! You've forgotten their name! Eros in Aries adores the chase and the thrill of making a maximum impact. That first falling-in-love phase is like heaven to you. But then your contradictory ('so self-aware, so full of shit') Gemini Sun kicks in. A hint of 'Where were you last night?' and you go demoning off into the sunset.

Cosmic flash: Your soulmate has an even lower boredom threshold than you. He/she changes the subject before you.

### TAURUS

Your Taurean Eros (lusty, robust, dependable) attracts people who are totally unlike the Gemini ideal. Your Sun in Gemini likes mind-gaming and manipulative, complicated conversations. You specialize in triple entendres and multilayered flirtations. But Eros in Taurus indicates a more traditional love nature. Those who are drawn to your steady Taurean side get a hell of a fright when they confront your 'don't fence me in' Gemini self.

To do: In your rush to bedazzle the latest 'victim', try not to tell more than three fibs.

### GEMINI

Sun and Eros in Gemini? Do you have a social secretary simply to handle all the requests for dates? A shrink on standby to counsel the broken hearts? You are alarmingly charismatic. This combo also gives you the gift of being light-hearted in love. Laughter and wit are your turn-ons. You're able to 'kiss the joy as it flies', preferring the fleeting beautiful moment to the day-in-day-out doldrums of domesticity.

Celestial love lesson: To stop exercising your skills by setting your heart on romancing monstrosities just as a challenge.

## CANCER

You'll come to their emotional rescue. At least, that's how your Cancerian Eros manifests itself to potential lovers. You're so adept at talking about your feelings, intuiting the unspoken demands of your partner, ultra in touch with where you're at. Running an emotionally responsible relationship is important to you. Yeah, and then there's your Sun in Gemini side — blessed (cursed) with the lowest boredom threshold on earth and loathing any kind of interaction that is not informative or amusing.
Stellar spell: Own up to this ASAP.

## LEO

Given your urbane and glossy surface gleam, nobody need ever know about your secret persona of true romantic. Yes, that's right! Your Sun in Gemini treats love as a game. Life is your laboratory and you're interested in people's drooling, practically Pavlovian responses to your gorgeousness. But Eros in Leo indicates a person who believes utterly in love. This part of you wants to swoon. So you're into both elegant detachment (Gemini) and the idea of hopeless devotion (Leo). Now you know.
Your 'type': A superstar.

## VIRGO

As both Gemini and Virgo are mind-centred, observational signs, you could be at risk of analyzing yourself out of love. You see everything! From that teensy white lie to the ill-dyed hair. You believe in love but insist on what you call discrimination. Would you accept that your standards are pretty extreme? You can also be at risk of letting your gregarious Gemini self embarrass your Eros in Virgo and then the Virgoan side of you overcompensates by guilting you.
What to do: Evoke the energy of Water: ocean, spa, pure emotion.

### LIBRA

With the Sun in Gemini and Eros in Libra, you like love that takes your mind to new places. True romance is, to you, inextricably linked with the expansion of your personal horizons. Art and creativity are always close at hand when you're smitten.

Cosmic flash: You are highly likely to meet your soulmate by following some form of artistic bliss! As Gemini and Libra are such compatible signs, you have few internal conflicts.

Potential ick factor: You could be in danger of over-intellectualizing romance. Airy-fairy? Ground yourself.

### SCORPIO

Your Gemini self is adept at light-hearted love. When the scenario turns turgid, your motto is 'Let's move on' and you do! But the part of you that is Eros in Scorpio desires intensity and profound level communication. Gemini can take or leave love. Scorpy has the potential to be completely compulsive-obsessive about even the most casual of affairs. So you say you want to keep things casual and then call 10 times a day.

What to do: Accept that this is an officially complicated dynamic. Try not to swing wildly between the extremes.

### SAGITTARIUS

Sun in Gemini with Eros in Sagittarius? You need space and stacks of it. Your ideal lover could even be in another country. Maybe he/she outdoes you by only letting you have the mobile phone number. You never get to see where they live and that suits you. Mystery and distance intrigue you big-time. You often set things up so that your relationship has automatic and frequent time apart. Your seduction style is full-on swashbuckling; you like to blow in with a blast of big ideas and political ranting and then disappear — poof! — unexpectedly.

## CAPRICORN

Gemini scorns convention. Capricorn covets it. So what to do when you have Sun in Gemini and Eros in Capricorn? You get over your hobby of falling in love with people who will be psychologically tormented by your very existence. Assuming that any relationship will be a soap opera, you reserve the best roles for yourself, casting your lover as gimped authoritarian figure whilst you stalk around looking amazing, with everyone in love with you and your crap.

Astro karma drama: This occurs when you meet someone like you.

## AQUARIUS

You're sensational, the sort of person who can change someone's life just by walking into a room and then out again. You're ultra ahead of your time, free spirited and a natural-born individualist. Your Sun in Gemini and Eros in Aquarius synergize beautifully together. There are no major contradictions between your Core Persona and Love Drives.

Celestial love glitch: You can get too caught up in personal fabulosity to actually pair-bond. Or your relationships wind up sibling-combative, sexless 'friendly' affairs.

## PISCES

You don't mean to mess with people's minds — you just can't help it. Your base impulse is to beguile everyone. You do this more or less innocently but with devastating efficiency. Then, once said person is utterly enchanted, you lost interest. They ring up for a date. You say you feel stalked. Admit it. You like them to be hard to get, preferably impossible. Your Sun in Gemini is contrary and Eros in Pisces cherishes the highest, over-the-top ideals of love. Normal everyday relating gets in the way of your fantasies.

To do: Get real.

# Or your Psyche is in...

### ARIES

Psyche in Aries can't help but be combative in love; it takes a special person to break through your barriers. But Sun in Gemini likes to project as carefree and light-hearted, a kind of wandering minstrel of love. So picture this: the part of you that's sparkling Gem doesn't give a damn whether a certain someone calls back or not. It's like, 'whatever'. But your Psyche-in-Aries self sees all romantic activity as a challenge. Getting to grips with this inner drama of yours awakens soulmating potential. Anger management?

### TAURUS

Only boring people get bored and nobody has ever accused you of being boring. Infuriating, yes. Amoral? Probably. Sun in Gemini craves non-stop novelty and variety. So you upset a few mediocrities in your quest for the new ... it happens. But perhaps you are repressing a vital aspect of yourself? This Psyche placement is a part of you forever, Taurus! So you do require a degree of stability. Part of your life needs to run along sensible lines. Cosmic flash: For you, gardening is spiritual.

### GEMINI

With your Sun and Psyche in Gemini, you are so multifaceted. It could even be that you're more comfortable with multiple realities! You zoom straight from the gym to cocktails without batting an eyelid. You're a multitasker, determined to extract every iota of value from each moment. So, what about love? You can be perversely drawn to people who would diss you for being so flexi-minded. You need someone as multi-everythinged as you.

## CANCER

You're a hard-boiled cynic who cries during nature documentaries. Why couldn't the cameraman have done something? Gemini skims merrily across the surface of the most turgid scenario. You enlighten life with quips or amoral observations. But your Cancerian Psyche is the most sensitive of all! You're empathetic, compassionate and often too perceptive for duller-witted people. Cosmic tasks: To get over the idea that being a feeling person undermines your mental sophistication. Mentor the shy.

## LEO

Charisma Central: you're too much for many people and this makes you happy. You'd rather fly fabulously solo than dumb down for anyone. There is something showbizzy about your love performance, sorry, love life. Blessed with the gift of living fully in the moment, carpe diem is your motto.
Karma drama: When you lose yourself in your own genius, so busy putting the spin on your latest hilarious anecdote that you do not notice your lover's eyes glazing over as he/she calculates escape options. Fear? Being upstaged.

## VIRGO

Guilt, for Geminis, is an unknown emotion. You guys are cheerfully amoral, refusing to judge or to be judged. But for Psyche in Virgo, guilting is a core competency! You alternate between glib self-loving and way over-the-top neuroses about personal foibles.
Astro tip: For peace of mind, channel Virgo energies into decluttering and administrivia ... not into over-analysis of your alleged defects or (worse) love life. In love, you're part easygoing (Gemini) and part Virgoan perfectionist. Ideally, you express the best aspects of both signs.

## LIBRA

Lovely and beguiling as you no doubt are (your Psyche is ruled by Venus, the Goddess of Love and Beauty), you are an enigma … perhaps even to yourself. Never listen overly to those who would have you be more fixed in character. As a Sun Sign Gemini you're symbolized by the Twins. And your Libran Psyche tips back and forward in order to find perfect balance. You are all about making constant little adjustments to create harmony.

Astro alibi: You're not fickle. You're a flexible being, responding to the zeitgeist.

## SCORPIO

Geminis just want to have fun! Psyche in Scorpio wants to reunite with a soulmate from past lives, pair-bond and work through issues together. To Psyche in Scorpio, the relationship must be far more than the sum of its parts. Or why bother? You see love as an intense transformative experience. If it doesn't hurt, you're not doing it right. The idea of a whimsical dalliance is kryptonite to your super-person. You're not casual about anything, let alone something so important as love and sex.

To do: Lighten up ASAP. A bit?

## SAGITTARIUS

Sun in Gemini and Psyche in Sagittarius? Freedom fetish! Someone asking where you were all week feels like an unacceptable space invasion. You love that feeling of nobody knowing exactly where you are. You like to see yourself as an 'open book' but really you're a raving enigma, even to yourself.

Celestial love lesson: You're often so fulfilled by your own company and that of the cool people you meet on your adventures, that true love can pass you by altogether! Cultivate the gorm to be as daring emotionally.

## CAPRICORN

Your Gemini self is just so flip, free-minded and modern. Your Psyche in Capricorn mitigates against this part of yourself, adding a subtone of sober self-awareness (*très* useful for someone with the Sun in Gemini, actually) and uncommon sense. You ideally use this paradigm to create a secure foundation for your Gemini Sun to shine out from.

What could go off: This Psyche sign can be prone to undue melancholy or harsh self-carping. If this is you, engage your Gemini side to shrug and smirk 'Let's move on!'

## AQUARIUS

You're the space cadet of love! You like nothing better than an unknown relationship frontier to explore. Familiar terrain? It irks you. Anything which vibes a little too safe, suburban or just plain naff has you making a few flimsy excuses and oozing out that door. There is no contradiction between your Gemini Sun and Aquarian Psyche. That's challenging in that you could live way too much in your mind.

Astro karma drama: Swept off your pretty feet by an immensely thick chic physique, you are forced to become more feeling,

## PISCES

You have the Sun in Gemini and Psyche in Pisces! This combo has you highly likely to find true love via following your brilliant career bliss. It's true! It also makes you a beautiful femme/homme fatale type. You smash hearts with a tinkly little laugh. You care only for the one on your mind at that moment, until the moment he/she succumbs to your wicked wiles and becomes thus 'tedious'. Your fave lover is a figment of your fantasy-prone mind. Remember that both Gemini and Pisces are Twin signs. Your soulmate is scarily like you.

# If you are a Cancer...
## June 22 to July 23

Crabs like you (and US writer Hunter S Thompson) know that 'When the going gets weird, the weird turn pro'. One of the most amazing things about you is how you can totally freak out over a trivial irk yet remain calm and gracious under real pressure. Ruled by the Moon, you are empathetic, seductive and nurturing. Nobody creates an emotional comfort zone like you guys. Off-form? Okay, you are prone to power-sulking and the invisible guilt rays you emit can poison the atmosphere for months. But mood-swinger or not, if you're in that come-hithery frame of mind, few can resist you and your great big goobly bedroom eyes.

# and your Eros is in...

# How your Sun sign gets it on with Eros & Psyche

## ARIES

Your Cancerian Sun makes you a highly emotional person — the astro motto for Cancer is 'I feel'. But Eros in Aries counteracts your hyped feeling nature by marching up and, in effect, bellowing 'I'm here now! Let's get it on!' Your manner is so brash and direct: 'You want it, or not?' You freak yourself out! But fret not, it's just your Inner Ramzilla out for a romp. You're a lot less slushy than the 'typical' Crab. You freak out when you sense lack of respect. Celestial love lesson: Accept that part of yourself is a full-on philandering Don Juan/ita.

## TAURUS

Sun in Cancer — Eros in Taurus? Apart from the fact that you're undoubtedly highly sexed, you have a weird astro-fate thing going on. You could well wind up dating and mating within a certain social set more than once, you understand. You have fascinating frissons with apparently platonic friends and, no, the attraction is not going to dissipate with time. This combination makes you suave in love. The two signs involved are *très* compatible and you come across as deceptively calm and sane. Astro flash: You could give it all up for security.

## GEMINI

People sometimes say that Gemini is the sign of no feelings while, of course, your Cancerian Sun is all about *feelings*. Lots of feelings. Feelings expressed eloquently at the drop of a hat. Your Eros in Gemini is the trickster of love — manipulative, elusive and game-playing. Yes, you're all that beneath your Cancerian sensitivity so is it any wonder lovers freak out? They're busy trying to revenge-manipulate the Gemini You and then you go all guilting and emotive on them. Or they suddenly morph into a cold-hearted 'Do I know you?' Gemini type.

# Soulmating

## CANCER

Wow! How about this? Your Sun and Eros signs match, making you a scarily empathetic and sensitive lover.

Astro karma drama: You're so psychic, you could find it tricky to distinguish where you stop and another begins. Seek solo Q-space to restore personal energies on a regular basis. Seduction-wise, you know in the first five seconds whether you and Mr/Ms Prospective are destined to spend any time together. Oddly, for someone who is so attuned to feelings, you can sometimes be what you euphemistically refer to as the 'victim' of your moods.

## LEO

You're interested in emotional interplay. A sentimentalist, you consider honouring the feelings of another to be the most vital aspect of any love affair. Cool, but your Eros in Leo is something else again. It's the part of you that longs to stalk into any room, dazzling all with sheer chic, full-on repartee and general personal hotness. An integral part of you doesn't give a damn about the emotions, unless they're part of your act.

What to do: Try not screaming 'Cut!' if someone's 'performance' irks you or appears not to be following your plot.

## VIRGO

Tradition, ceremony and family — the combination of a Cancerian Sun with Eros in Virgo makes them vital to you. You like things to be done right. You can't for a moment warm to someone whom you disapprove of. Actually, you can't get aroused with crumbs in the bed. Your ethical standards sustain you throughout what can be a tumultuous early mating history.

Astro karma drama: You can be so-o-o attracted to those 'naughty' (that is, dysfunctional) people whom you feel you ought to rescue. You do this even against their will!

## LIBRA

Cancerian Sun and Libran Eros? With this placement, you may not want to even know what you're feeling. Eros in Libra cares about elegance, harmony and eloquence. You could have no qualms suppressing any ugly or messy emotions that seem to get in the way of your *dolce vita* ideal. And yet, for true happiness, you need to feel free to gush forth emotion whenever you want. Romancing relaxes you — you're the most suave of seducers, then you give adorees a hell of a fright by unleashing your true self.

To do: Create an authentic you.

## SCORPIO

Cancer and Scorpio are both Water signs so you're predominantly a Water person: creative, artistic and comfortable with depths of emotion some might consider oceanic, overwhelming. To say that you are a true romantic is to understate the situation. Vow now to never try and conduct a love affair with someone who begrudges his/her love or tries to make out like it's casual. You deserve — and are destined for — a soulmating.

Astro flash: Being so Watery, you do need to 'dry out' some of the sogginess via a dose of sanguine thought.

## SAGITTARIUS

Cancerian Sun and Eros in Saggo? Hmmm. These are two of the most disparate signs of all. You're a sensitive, home-loving Cancerian but your love persona is that of wanderlusty and extroverted Sagg! If smitten, you may project a personality that is completely different from the real you. You may be a bit messed up but you sure as hell are lucky in love! Being double blessed by Jupiter and the Moon exerts a protective energy in love.

Cosmic love flash: You can be both amusing as well as emotionally with-it, did you know?

# Soulmating

## CAPRICORN

You go on gut instincts. Eros in Capricorn weighs up shoes (expensive?), the body (worked out), the hair (kempt?) and innumerous other little factors on the patented Capricorn Suitability Index. For example, someone mentions a little tax debt to you and the rating falls. Mum's a neurosurgeon? Up it goes again. Oh, it all sounds so harsh, but it really *is*! You can skip some sensational romantic experiences by being so hung up on the material-security reality.

Astro weirding: Eros in Cap hates that your Cancerian self is so touchy-feely. You worship competence.

## AQUARIUS

Does anyone have the map to your mind? It's like a labyrinth in there. As a Sun Sign Cancerian, you're emotionally complex, *très* profound and so-o-o sentimental. Aquarius, the sign of your Eros, signifies the Higher Mind and futuristic-thought style. This is a beautiful (and unusual) combination and you are likely *très* talented and alluring. But learning to use this scenario is akin to handling an expensive sports car. Yes, you're highly strung! Cosmic flash: Don't ever try to do just mind or heart. It's both.

## PISCES

Your Eros in Pisces makes you prone to fantasy and idealized visions of romance. Combine these two traits with that sentimental Cancerian Sun and, voila! The love machine! You consider relationships to be an art, not a science and you don't listen to a word anyone (or any article) tells you about it. Yearning for your soulmate from the second you hear your first love story, you follow your heart with fascinating results. You give excellent seasoned romantic advice.

Potential ick factor: You're a mood-swinger extraordinaire.

# Or your Psyche is in...

## ARIES

Drama-Queenie? Technically, Cancer (your Sun Sign) and Aries (your Psyche sign) are radically different. Cancer is ruled by the Moon while Aries comes under macho Mars. Cancer is considered one of the most feminine signs of all and Aries is traditionally masculine. But, guess what they have in common? Both signs love a good scene. Your Cancerian Sun is as moody as hell — freedom to change your mind is a prerequisite for your happiness. And Psyche in Aries enjoys clearing the air — dramatically.

## TAURUS

This combo signifies one of the most accomplished seducers of all. It's not that you go around pouncing on people — you are too subtle for that. It's that they spend five seconds in your company and never want to leave. You have an innate knack of making others not just at ease, but understood like never before. You're sophisticated enough to not let on all that you've gleaned. The dark side? You can vibe possessive re your partner's other friends.

## GEMINI

As a Sun sign Cancerian, you're in tune with your heart, able to recognize, articulate and process feelings. But your Psyche in Gemini doesn't want to know. No matter how sky-high your EQ (Emotional Intelligence), there is an aspect of you that just wants to be amused. This astro energy is tricky to handle.

What to do: Don't beat up an emotion when it doesn't exist. Accept you sometimes need frivolity and to feel pleasantly shallow or flip. Humour, like honey, catches more 'flies'.

# Soulmating

## CANCER

Your Sun and your Psyche are both Cancerian! Happily, your core persona (the Sun) is identical to your secret soul persona as symbolized by Psyche. This placement is often linked to the ability to express emotions and thoughts via art or music.

Astro karma drama: You could feel inclined to throw your beautiful self (creative/psychic gifts and all) at someone who simply does not (and will never) get you. Don't!

Cosmic challenges: Moving on from the past graciously. Dismantling the shrine to your ex-lover.

## LEO

The person with the Sun in Cancer is happy to exist quietly behind the scenes. The murmured appreciation of a grateful few are enough. You value chez you and the peaceful life. Okay, so that's part of the lovely you. But then there's your Psyche in Leo! This is the aspect of you craving the limelight, who won't leave the house without perfect hair or a full face of make-up and simply must be honoured en masse, sweetie.

Cosmic lesson: To learn to love your inner diva. Hair homage is always a good start.

## VIRGO

You are capable of immense compassion. You'd rather go with the emotional flow than get hung up on the details. Aha! Your Psyche sign is Virgo, the details fetishist. Do you find that, no matter how immersed in the moment you may be, part of you is forever making little lists? Or objectively analyzing the situation? That's your Psyche in Virgo and, though it is the source of so much of your genius (most people are not as observant), you must not let it cramp Cancerian flow — that is, the ability to express emotion without hyperventilating.

## LIBRA

Entrepreneurial and canny as it is (and are you), your Cancerian Sun is about spontaneity of feeling. Great! But your Psyche in Libra doesn't trust that sort of thing. Libra thinks everything goes much better with stage management — that is, the right lighting, a little styling, properly rehearsed lines. You understand? So part of you just wants to emote. Another aspect of you needs things to be 'done right'. Your Psyche in Libra goes crazy if not acknowledged. Keep her happy via scent, flowers, body lotions.

## SCORPIO

Tantalizing and elusive, you are adept at managing your love life. Psyche in Scorpio lends a certain steely strength to your Cancerian Sun, whilst bolstering the already-present highly refined perceptions. You are the ultimate confidante and the accuracy of your advice astounds.

Potential ick factor: You can be insanely manipulative — setting would-be lovers secret little 'tests', imagining far-out conspiracies and/or flying into a flip-out at some faux slight.

What to do: Tame psycho-dramatic tendencies ASAP.

## SAGITTARIUS

As a Sun Sign Cancerian, you are preoccupied with scoring security (emotional, material, whatever). Your life is all about being in the comfort zone. But Psyche in Sagittarius screeches 'Don't fence me in!' Yes, a *très* important part of you is actually quite different from the core persona aka Sun-sign you! You just want to say 'Stuff it' and fly off to some beautiful secluded beach. You want to rant out opinions that aren't all about shoring up security needs and the status quo.

Astro flash: Wilderness getaways and sports will heal your soul more than you imagine.

# Soulmating

## CAPRICORN

Psyche in Capricorn adds a worldly dimension to your oft-intuitive Cancerian Sun. And it is, in fact, this mature edge that saves you from classic feelings-driven acts of idiocy such as letting your compassion lure you into a relationship with some dysfunctional vampire. Capricorn can see the creature coming a block away and takes evasive action. So, don't guilt yourself the next time you have a strong self-preservation instinct even if it does seem a bit harsh and material. Like money, for instance. It's your secret Capricorn soul looking out.

## AQUARIUS

Loving those blissful bonding moments, your Cancerian Sun murmurs 'Hold me' to the lover. Then you get the giggles. That's your Psyche in Aquarius kicking in. It's the part of you that feels embarrassed at intimacy and hits the roof when you can't do exactly as you please. But it is also the part of you that's avant-garde and open-minded. You may not exactly want to hang out with people in general (they get on your nerves) but, then again, you sure stick up for their rights.

Astro flash: Alternative forms of healing are lucky for you.

## PISCES

Your Sun (in Cancer) and your Psyche (in Pisces) are both Water signs! So you're at home in the realms of feeling and highly likely to have artistic talent. You're also prone to passive aggression, driving the more direct types who are always so drawn to you absolutely bonkers! Ideally, you learn to express angst or rage without being totally chaotic about it. Or not? Your Psyche in Pisces adds some tolerance and broad-mindedness to your Cancerian compassion. You find it truly hard to judge and, as a result, you are Mr/Ms Popularity.

# If you are a Leo...
## July 24 to August 23

'I was born with sophistication and sex appeal,' boasted legendary Leo Mae West, perhaps speaking for all Lion folk. Glam, inspirational and big-hearted, you are the performance artistes of the Zodiac. The neo-Leo life is an epic production. It may have a cast of thousands, but Leo is always the producer, director and star. To the theatrical mindset, critics don't count. Only the applause matters. Leos don't walk into a room. They make an entrance. Their bathroom is more akin to a dressing room. They are always on stage. Off-form, our Leo is vain, pompous and a pathological attention seeker. The astro motto for Leo is 'I rule.'

# and your Eros is in...

# Soulmating

### ARIES

There is only one star sign as egomaniacal as Leo and that's Aries. Your syrupy charm is overwritten by the direct approach of Ramzilla. Rather than the slithering, glamorous seduction of the Leo cliché, the lines are suddenly along the lines of 'Well, are we going to do this or what?' The self-regarding regality of the Leo mixed with the athletic directness of the Aries is a potent force and the result is a highly successful pouncing bounder.

To do: Forget the figure for a moment. Could your bloated ego benefit from fasting?

### TAURUS

Leo loves to be the best — at everything! And Eros in Taurus just *has* to be the best in bed. Combining the Big Cat's haughty fabulosity with a ruttish Eros influence, you are a totally fascinating hybrid. The Taurus Eros could easily manifest — in Leo — as a desire to dress up for your bedroom performance, or even a willingness to commit your incredibleness to film! Taurus Eros is about the unashamed enjoyment of one's body; Leo is always thinking of hair. When they reside in one person you can expect some boudoir theatre.

### GEMINI

Imagine a larger-than-life, theatrically alluring creature who swans into the party and transfixes all who go there. It's you! You're beloved by everyone and warm instantly to those who attract you. This is the classic Leo pose. But add the tricky and troublesome Eros in Gemini and your MO (Modus Operandi) is about going off a lover even before anything has happened. You're all gush, hype and compliments when the show is actually on. But, in the morning, it's like 'Sorry, but do I know you?' Watch this!

Astro karma drama: Someone does it back to you!

## CANCER

The temperamental star? You are a fabulous and accomplished trouper with massive lashings of self-confidence and belief in your innate amazingness. Add that to your somewhat needier Eros-in-Cancer influence and run for cover! You can't help but be tempestuous and prone to dramatic scenes. The saggy waitress (unfairly) serves the table next to you first? It's all on. Doesn't she know who you are? You're the ultimate mega-maintenance diva, combining clingy emotions with high-demand ego.

To do: Give back to 'your people'.

## LEO

The central joke of the Eros-in-Leo love style is that everything is a show and your part in it is the star turn. This falls in with the Leo personality that demands theatricality in all that they do. Potential lovers who are shy or overly modest could be quite intimidated by double Leo you. Mind you, such a person might be mistaken for the help by our regal one. You are a person who is never really off the stage.

Your seduction-pursuit style: It can be like revisiting the signature lines from a lot of very bad movies.

## VIRGO

Wow! Are your suitors in for a big surprise! Sucked in by the classic Leo glitz, hype and dazzle, they suddenly get hit with fusspotty Eros in Virgo! Your Leo self luxuriates in the moment of love, the sensation of mutual regard and that gaze 'held just a fraction too long' kind of stuff. Eros in Virgo notes the slight stutter, misuse of a pronoun and gulping of wine. Can you turn Eros in Virgo off for a moment? No!

Cosmic love task: To recognize that your standards are ludicrous! Don't drop someone for having split ends!

# Soulmating

## LIBRA

You're so in love with yourself that any interloper from the outside (aka a romantic partner) feels like a kinky threesome. You almost get guilty about betraying yourself with another. Yet the irony of beautiful You is that you pull non-stop. The queue forms wherever you are that particular day! Your Leo charisma and Eros-in-Libra charm is irresistible to all but those who've already dated someone like you. You can keep applicants dangling for decades, too dithery or self-obsessed to give them an honest answer, unwilling to narrow options.

## SCORPIO

Leos know that the show must go on. Just as long as it's their show. So what happens when a luvvie Leo has Eros in Scorpio? A great deal of intensity in romantic pursuits, a lot of toxic paranoia about how much you are divulging and a desire to mate with one other for the rest of eternity. Eros in Scorp takes love very seriously. It adds a deeper and more profound dimension to garishly glamorous Leo You, with your serial mass-seductions and air of self-importance.

Astro flash: Could family introduce you to your true love?

## SAGITTARIUS

Imagine two people who are both brassy about life. While one likes to be out flitting from one experience to another, the other person prefers to limit their adventures to locations where they are the centre of attention. So it goes with you! Eros in Saggo likes crowded hours and whirlwind romances in new places. But the Leo side of the equation is far more fixed about having special space where the Leonine specialness can shine.

Astro joke: Saggo tactlessness and social gaffes are sure to puncture big Leo's pomposity.

## CAPRICORN

One of the best things that can ever happen to a Leo is having something in their life that balances up the fabulosity and ego enough to make them functional. And, you've also got Eros in Capricorn! You're dazzling, talented and sophisticated. Capricorn mops up Leo excess and adds extra discriminating savvy. You lot can allow vanity to lure you into ludicrous love affairs. For example, the octogenarian matinee idol and the late-teens showgirl. But, this Eros sign keeps you strictly sane.

Most likely: To be successful and so admired.

## AQUARIUS

Wondering why you find it hard relating to the suave, self-assured (up themselves) Leos of legend? Your Eros is in Aquarius, which is the opposite sign to Leo! The Big Cat loves to touch — some would even say 'feel up'. And, while Aquarius can't stand physical intimacy in public, Leos are socially warm. Unless they feel they are in compatible company, Aquarians are renowned for their sangfroid. Ideally, you gotta learn to love your Aquarius side. It makes you (sssh) much more aware, cool and progressive than the typical Leo.

## PISCES

A star is born. And reborn! Every day you wake up and reinvent yourself, after taking the requisite contemplation time for tuning into the Universe, of course. Artistic talent, spiritual yearnings and desirability are your currency in love, in everything. You're a delicately calibrated blend of other-worldly concerns and real-politik ambition. Your true love must really get both these aspects, not merely one. For example, the relationship with that yoga guru won't last if they've got daggy hair.

Astro flash: Don't resent pragmatic reality and you'll truly shine.

# Or your Psyche is in...

### ARIES

What happens when the schmoozy, high-touch-factor Leo is influenced by the volatile Psyche in Aries? You should know! The Leo You loves to build consensus, to seduce agreement out of people. But your secret love nature is combative and belligerent in disagreements. In the right (crappy) mood, you can escalate anything — even a compliment — into a psycho-theatrical scene. Astro blessing: You take your authentic star quality for granted.

### TAURUS

Leo's secret daggy side? With Psyche in Taurus, you've certainly got one. Sure, you seldom reveal it to your public but you like slothing out on the couch with a pile of carbs and a steady supply of plonk to watch less-than-salubrious television. As Taurus is an Earth sign, this is literally a *très* grounding influence on Leo hubris. Stressed? Getting into the garden or any form of greenery will always calm those diva nerves.
Love weirding: You're happy with someone who loves daggy you.

### GEMINI

Leo is the king/queen of the jungle. Psyche in Gemini can't stand to be told what to do. You're so bolshie and wayward! Gemini is the sign of communicators and Leo's all about self-expression. You are a natural performer, writer, poet or chronicler of life. You may well have a startling faculty for words and should certainly pen love letters whenever you have the chance or correct inspiration.
Your muse: A man or woman who's completely changeable. You like to be kept guessing and amused.

## CANCER

Ready for the highly sentimental version of the Leo? The energy of Psyche in Cancer brings a sometimes tricky aspect to your Leo love nature. Whereas Leo likes to keep things light and showy, Psyche in Cancer is far more suited to hoarding feelings, sulking and wanting to endlessly discuss the 'Us'. Luckily, if this fits with Leo's psychodrama du jour, then the desire to pick apart and analyze the relationship can be filtered very much through the luvvie Leo prism.

Astro flash: You could easily skew to ancestor-worship.

## LEO

The planets align! When the outward Big Cat matches the secret inner Leo love nature, what do we get? The potential to make all relationships from marriage to casual conquests a total drama trip. Leos are showy anyway, but with Psyche in Leo the urge to bring flowers, put on a show, write poems and pledge undying love becomes an absolute necessity.

Astro flash: Don't let anyone trample on your beautiful neo-Leo dreams! You're a natural-born creative person with the talents (and temperament!) to prove it.

## VIRGO

Hmm. Your Sun in Leo likes the big picture — that part of you is only too happy just glossing over stupid details. You'll wing it on the night, trusting your own glib beauty and charisma to fill in any gaps. But Psyche in Virgo is all about the minutiae of life ... and love! Your Psyche in Virgo is that insistent little voice inside of you whispering on about budgetary concerns and correct form. Yes, it drives you gaga and gets in the way of your Leonine greatness but honouring it is also the way to true fabulosity. So, next time, make sure you listen.

## LIBRA

Sun in Leo with Psyche in Libra? You're surely an official catch. Perhaps even an official beauty? You're so Sun-Venus influenced that you've probably been sought after from an early age. Weren't you the Mr/Ms Popularity in first grade? The issue with this placement is not coasting along on your charm! If you're a little over-smarmy, ease the sleaze!

To do: Practise following through on what you say you'll do. Leos know exactly what they want — Libra can be *très* indecisive. You ideally learn to accept this about yourself.

## SCORPIO

Your Psyche in Scorpio makes you heaps deeper than the classic Leo: you're more perceptive (to the extent that you are highly likely to be psychic) and interested in alternative theories about reality. Whereas the Leo part of you is only interested in one reality. That's right, *you*. Yours. Yourself. So you're a more evolved Leo, a neo-Leo. But the problem here is that both Leo and Scorpio are what we call 'Fixed' signs. You need to take extra efforts not to become stuck.

To do: Practise embracing something new each day.

## SAGITTARIUS

The future is here and it looks like fun! Thus thinks your ever-optimistic and youthful Psyche in Sagittarius. You're forever youthful and in motion. With this Psyche sign and Sun combo, no matter what happens you will always be able to tune into a bubbling little fountain of hope and positivity. You could also be slightly over the top, of course. You are a highly fiery, extroverted and gregarious person (No? Then you are repressing your Psyche sign!) and can exhaust other people.

Astro hint: Be more receptive. Lots more.

## CAPRICORN

Who's the most likely to succeed then? Your Psyche in Capricorn could irk you immensely as you fret over whether or not you are rich enough, thin enough, respected enough, successful enough and so on. But, wow! Do you make it fast! The combo of being a super-glam Sun sign Leo with Psyche in Capricorn — the most ambitious sign of all — is almost unbeatable.

Weirdo astro karma drama: Despite all the social genius and brilliant career scheming, you could have a secret thing for really unsuitable types.

## AQUARIUS

Wow! Complicated or what! Leo and Aquarius are opposite signs of the Zodiac. When your Sun and Psyche signs are in opposition, you get a dynamic personal tension syndrome operating within you! To be avoided: Stalemating. Getting too stuck at either end of the opposition. You ideally learn how to both be Leonine (outgoing, showbizzy, generous, glam) and to honour your more inner Aquarian Psyche self. How to do it? By being ahead of your time, in touch with alternate realities and emancipated.

## PISCES

Both your Sun and Psyche signs (Leo and Pisces) signify the beautiful dreamer. You are a creative soul and don't let anyone tell you otherwise. Romantic and extremely seductive, you are more than adequately equipped for love.

Astro glitch: You're *so* idealistic and the more mundane aspects of everyday loving could leave you feeling lukewarm, searching for fresh thrills or to revisit the throes of new loving. You ideally learn to make even the 'dull' stuff fun and pleasurable, as opposed to mindless pleasure seeking. Also, your love of manipulations and mind games may not be as much fun for your lover.

# If you are a Virgo...
## August 24 to September 23

You're helpful, witty, suave and polite. But you're also prone to what you think of as 'correctional motivation' — aka nagging. You agree with fellow Virgo Leo Tolstoy (FYI: an amazing proportion of well-known writers are born under the sign of Virgo) that 'true life is lived when tiny changes occur'. You are a work in progress, always tweaking something or other. Your astro motto is 'I analyze': you do indeed have honed powers of observation and discrimination that are ideally not turned to the Virgoan off-form traits of fuss-pottery, guilting and nit-pickery. You benefit immensely from a little less use of those famed critical faculties and a bit more time for reverie in your life.

# and your Eros is in...

# How your Sun sign gets it on with Eros & Psyche

## ARIES

The Sun in Virgo with Eros in Aries? Do you glow in the dark? Yes, you're a sensible and suave little Virgo, able to be taken anywhere, productive and sane and always functional. But your Arian Eros is what turns you into a love monster. Eyes lock across the room ... or it's just you and Mr/Ms Spesh who seem to get the joke and you're off. Eros in Aries is all about conquest and heat. You love to feel that buzz and, frankly, this part of you could sometimes be an embarrassment to your more straitlaced and shy Virgo Sun. But so what? The famous Aries blowhardery can annihilate that innate Virgoan modesty.

## TAURUS

Both Virgo and Taurus are Earth signs, which means they are pragmatic and sensual. Oddly enough, this combo is most likely to be turned on by people utterly unlike you. You are inextricably drawn to complicated, game-playing creatures of allure but little libido. They like to mess with your hard-won Earth-sign stability. Are you over this phase yet? The only real conflict between your Virgo and Taurus side is this: Virgo is easily aroused by intelligence and likes to seduce accordingly. Taurus is purely physical ... you need both brains and beauty!

## GEMINI

Astro destiny: To fall in love via following your brilliant career bliss. Your soulmate could even be someone with whom you form a business. An overling? Underling? Both your Virgo Sun and Gemini Eros are ruled by Mercury, trickster of the gods and the planet-ruling intellect. So communication is absolutely vital to you. No matter how divine looking or adoring the potential lover, if there's no mental spark between you guys you find it impossible to get even remotely interested.

# Soulmating

## CANCER

Your Virgo side prides itself on being logical. Your Cancerian Eros does not give a damn about logic, received opinion or anything but its own emotions at the time. And, wow! What emotions! If you've ever wondered why, as a Virgo, you are so prone to being overwhelmed with strong feelings, here is your answer.

Astro clue that you could be neglecting your Eros: You dream of water — raging flash floods, tidal waves, torrential rain. You ideally combine that Virgo uncommon sense with Cancerian intuition and emotional intelligence.

## LEO

Okay, so there's you — sensible, suave Virgo — and then there's this eccentric egomaniac that seems to emerge whenever love is involved. Virgo, meet your Eros in Leo. It's like your Sun sign wants to find out more about the person (background, parents, life goals, any addictions, etc) whilst Eros in Leo is rushing out to purchase airline tickets for travel to romantic places, composing love poetry or turning up at dawn to serenade the object of desire. Repressing Eros is pointless.

To do: Find ways of letting your Leo out every day.

## VIRGO

Sun and Eros in Virgo! At least you don't spin people out by coming on all strong in one mode and then proving to be a completely different person. No, you're *très* clear about who and what you are. You're a perfectionista, showing the rest of us just how sexy it is to be productive and sane.

The potential ick factor? You could be over-critical of both yourself and would-be lovers. You're a double Virgo! Next time you find yourself crossing someone off your cocktail party list because of (say) their poor grammar, think again.

## LIBRA

As a Sun sign Virgo, you tend to demonstrate love via being practical and helpful. For example, you remember what book someone said they wanted to read and pick it up for them. You are one of the best long-term lovers of all — familiarity actually turns you on. But romantic gesturing is not you. You often think flowers et al are cheap and tacky. Okay, but your Eros in Libra really loves all that stuff. Moonlight, gorgeous gifts of scent, red roses, cute little 'I love you snookums' personalized dating rituals and love song requests. Admit it!

## SCORPIO

You're so intense! The combination of Sun in Virgo with Eros in Scorpio makes you quietly charismatic, hypnotically alluring. But not to everyone. You polarize people. They are likely to have strong reactions to you either way, you understand. Dislike? They'll ring ahead to check that you're not going to be at a party before rasping. Like? They'll adore you forever and a day, refusing to hear a word against you. Your psyched-up love and romance style freaks out the conservative Virgo you, of course...
To do: Find a suave Scorp role model.

## SAGITTARIUS

Finally! The explanation you have been waiting for. Yes, you are a Virgo. But your Eros in Sagittarius is all about escape. You yearn to just do it, to just go! Whilst your Sun in Virgo slogs away, ticking off the bills as they are paid, responding dutifully to all emails, your Saggo Eros is fantasizing about blowing all the rent money on a junket to Tahiti. Whilst your Virgoan side feels smug and self-congratulatory about all the productivity, Sagg thinks 'This is my life'...
Karma drama: You attract people who awaken Saggability.

## CAPRICORN

With the Sun in Virgo and Eros in Capricorn, art is oddly important to your romantic life. Your soulmate somehow shares your cultural ideas or perhaps you even meet through a some creative pursuit? You may even admire their work. Virgo and Capricorn are intensely compatible signs so it is unlikely you have any major internal conflict going on here except that you can overdo the prerequisites for seeking Mr/Ms Right. You automatically rule out whole tribes of people whereas you are so extended and uplifted by being more open-minded.

## AQUARIUS

Sun in Virgo and Eros in Aquarius? This is so often the combo of people who are good writers or photographers, eccentrics and alternative health converts. And you? Both Virgo and Aquarius share an interest in others and their life choices; you are bound to have a vast, eclectic bunch of friends. In love you find it almost impossible to warm up for anyone who you think of as thick or a dullard. Even in love you can be cruel should you think your lover is dumbing down for any reason. You may well be the most eccentric 'dark horsie' Sun-Eros combo of all.
To do: Be more comfy with intimacy.

## PISCES

Here we go! Your Sun in Virgo believes in two people in a mature relationship bonding by shared beliefs and goals. Your Eros in Pisces believes in twin souls reuniting after lifetimes spent apart. Your Sun in Virgo believes in what is in front of you such as information from trusted sources. Eros in Pisces believes in unicorns and foes. Their druid song stays on your mind. Both of these two extremes are you! You will only find true romance once you own up to your Eros in Pisces. Soulmating is you!

# Or your Psyche is in...

## ARIES

As a Sun Sign Virgo, your core competency is modesty. You're often so unaware of your better qualities. How you manage to combine this with your martyr skills is an astrological mystery. But, the Virgo vibe is ameliorated by Psyche in Aries, an influence that will not let a single achievement go unsung. This is a great combo; when Virgo feels put upon, your Aries acts as cheer squad. To do: Accept that you've got an ego happening and buff it up!

## TAURUS

Virgo and Taurus are naturally compatible signs. Your Sun in Virgo finds it easy to understand your more inner Psyche in Taurus as both are Earth signs. You are blessed with a natural-born ability to heal and nurture yourself.

Astro tip: Psyche in Taurus benefits from exposure to nature and greenery. Get thee to the wilderness without letting your Virgo side guilt you into a long hike — and just be. Or take up gardening. Virgo can over-intellectualize. Your Psyche helps you detune.

## GEMINI

Did you know that Virgo is a Mutable sign? That is, you're flexi minded and able to accept change with ease. This is what will allow you to access the gifts of your Psyche in Gemini. For you to feel at ease, life ought to be evolving. Both your Virgo Sun and Psyche in Gemini like the minutiae of life, creating and re-creating routines, lifestyles, ideas du jour. In love, what you most fear is not abandonment or being alone but boredom.

To do: Start your autobiography.

# Soulmating

### CANCER

Your Sun in Virgo values logic and streamlined systems. Your Cancerian Psyche wants to put feeling first. You could flip back and forth between the two. What to do? Ideally, you let your Virgoan self balance any emotional extremes whilst letting Cancerian intuition enhance the Virgo thought style. Your Psyche sign is what allows you those sudden leaps of faith and instinct.

Astro destiny: Friends are fated. It feels like you've known them before and maybe you have.

Astro flash: Soulmate comes via friends?

### LEO

Psyche in Leo is the prima diva. There's a part of you that wants to make an entrance, hog the limelight and graciously acknowledge the applause. No? You may be too immersed in your Sun-in-Virgo vibe to be in touch with your Psyche sign. Yet, it is vital (for your spiritual wellbeing) that you tune into your Leo aspects.

Cosmic flash: Leo rules Hair and honouring your hair reality is always the quickest way to bring out any repressed Leonine aspects of yourself. More involved? Find your voice. Have you considered singing?

### VIRGO

Okay, so inner you and outer you make a perfect match. Beautiful! You are likely to especially embody the classic Virgoan attributes and be smart, witty, suave and polite. Of course, you are also thus more at risk of being an off-form Virgo — fusspotty, a guilter and hypochondriac. Eeek? Not at all. Fitness and nutrition are a really good way to antidote any excess of Virgo. Far better to be addicted to the gym or counting every single carbohydrate than to be in constant self-guilting mode.

Astro flash: Pisceans are good for you.

## LIBRA

Between your Virgoan Sun's analytical jags and Psyche in Libra's seesawing in order to find balance, you could be a *très* deep character indeed. This combo affords a light and sparkling intellect, innate charm and — often — dazzling beauty. Even if you are not officially an utter stunner, you project as if you are.

Celestial love lesson: Subliminal messages you give off draw a lot of people to you but the attraction may be only one way. So learn the art of the tactful brush-off. Feeling blue? Beauty treatments are Zen for you.

## SCORPIO

Adaptability is — or should be — your aim in life. As a Virgo, you're able to make sense of everyday complexities and, in fact, it's one of your joys in life! But Psyche in Scorpio can become rigid about change and communication. You're a deep thinker and probably prone to clairvoyant dreams, sudden little 'hunches' or even full-blown paranormal experiences. But true happiness depends on being more with-it on the mundane plane.

To do: Channel your witchy Scorpionic Psyche correctly by writing a dream journal.

## SAGITTARIUS

Wow! What a bundle of cute contradictions you must be. It's like you are both Bugs Bunny and Elmer Fudd! Your Sun in Virgo feels most content within clear-cut boundaries and following a routine. Your Psyche in Sagittarius is strictly free range, chafing at any kind of prescribed style of life. You find the fullest expression of happiness by not completely upsetting that Virgoan wish list but via succumbing to spontaneity, throwing over the sensible course of action from time to time.

Astro flash: Hang out with Saggos!

## CAPRICORN

An altruistic Virgo, you're motivated by self-interest at heart. Eeek? Not at all. If you have Psyche in Capricorn aligned with the Sun in Virgo, as you do, it's there for a reason. You are probably over-interested in others' lives, too ready to help out and so nice that you don't declare your own boundaries strongly enough. Psyche in Capricorn is the worldly and sophisticated part of you that says 'come on' to some bludger trying to take advantage of the quiet shy Virgoan You.

Astro witchery: So-called power-dressing strengthens your soul!

## AQUARIUS

Everyone wants to say they love you! But you're not listening. As a mixture of Sun in Virgo and Psyche in Aquarius, you're free-spirited, super-smart and progressive. But, yeah, you may not be mega-comfie with intimacy. Both Virgo and Aquarius are head-oriented signs and happiest in the realms of the intellect. Your Psyche in Aquarius is just brilliant for antidoting any over-judgmental tendencies of your Virgoan Sun.

To do: Activate your Psyche sign by reading up on alternative realities, politics, cuisine.

## PISCES

With Sun in Virgo and Psyche in Pisces you could feel as though an aspect of you is always whirring along to undo all your good work to date. Virgo and Pisces are astrological opposites, but guess what? They need each other. A Virgo with Psyche in Pisces is blessed. Your Virgo self is prone to overwork and self-guilting. Your Piscean Psyche is the part of you that forgives, forgets and lets you relax. It's the 'Life is good — let's party' you.

How to access it: Keep a dream journal. You could be amazed at how accurate you are.

# If you are a Libran...
## September 24 to October 23

You're born under the sign of the beautiful person. Ruled by Love Goddess Venus, your astro motto is 'I cooperate' and, you do! You are blessed with the ability to see both sides of any equation, which is probably where you get your reputation of being indecisive and dithery from. Known for your 'whim of steel', social climbing skills and occasional hypocrisy, you are also sweet, tactful, loving and charming. You agree with Libran great actress Sarah Bernhardt that 'we must live for the few who know and appreciate us, who judge and absolve us and for whom we have the same affection and indulgence.'

# and your Eros is in...

### ARIES

You're romantically sophisticated and an elegant passive-aggressive. Timing is your particular forte. The ugly, ill-thought spontaneous outburst is not for you. Another gift of your Sun in Libra is the ability to see all aspects of a scenario. You can detach from your own ego-driven viewpoint. So how do you go with Eros in Aries? Eros is the part of you which is brash, domineering and impulsive to the point of insanity. In courtship, you can inadvertently conceal your complexity. Do you seethe beneath that cute carapace of yours?

### TAURUS

In love, Libra is light-hearted and flirtatious, a master/mistress of the seductive arts. But your Sun in Libra is enhanced by Eros in Taurus, the only other sign of the Zodiac to be ruled by Venus. So? You're blessed with supernatural sex appeal as well as possibly one of the most maddening personalities in the solar system. Your Libran Sun specializes in dithering around an apparently bedazzling array of possibilities. Eros in Taurus picks a path and bulldozes through, no matter what.
Astro flash: 'Cleave to the sunnier side of doubt'.

### GEMINI

Both Libra and Gemini are Air signs; you're most likely sanguine, breezy and socially progressive. In fact, you are one of the most elegantly tolerant and least judgmental of all people. You have the gift of instantly enhancing the lives (and egos) of those lucky enough to be in your orbit.
Potential ick factor: Your Libran Sun is wowed by love and happiest when living life in tandem with a beloved other. Eros in Gemini can come across as a 'take it or leave it', person thus giving off the incorrect impression that you're fine flying solo.

## CANCER

Sun in Libra with a Cancerian Eros? This is officially tricky. Why? Because your Sun sign bestows on you the blessing of being cool-headed and civilized in love. You are easily able to repress uncomfortable or socially inconvenient feelings. For example, if you make a scene, it will probably be when you are looking officially fabulous. Yet your Eros is in Cancer which gives you a strong desire to simply express your emotions without even straining them through the sieve of social efficacy.

Cosmic love lesson: Not alternating between cloying and avoiding.

## LEO

Your astro destiny is to be sought after and adored, to never be alone and to always be in love. Yes, that's what you get with the Sun in Libra and Eros in lusty Leo. So, what's the catch? You could be adulation addicted and selfish, unable to truly give to another. Dependability may be a challenge to you. Ditto accepting a partner when he/she is in non-snazzy mode. You find it horrendously easy to beguile other people but true content comes once you move beyond mere ego gratification.

Cosmic serendipity: Long-time friend could become lover.

## VIRGO

As a Libran with Eros in Virgo, you probably need more solo quality time than you imagine. Your Libran self appreciates more or less non-stop company. You may even think that you are afraid to be alone. But you benefit big time from taking that space to yourself. You may need it to sort out your so-irritating contradictions. Your Libran self is a beauty lover, you have aesthetic standards that must be met for you to feel anything ... but Eros in Virgo likes brains.

Astro flash: You are SO hard to please! Too hard?

# Soulmating

### LIBRA

You're a double Libran! Bossy and beautiful, you take the concept of 'lifestyle' seriously. Happily, there is no conflict between your core persona and the you that is aroused the moment you're romantically turned on. As you seduce is how you are. You make love your highest priority in life. You're capable of throwing over anything or anybody to follow your romantic bliss.

Potential ick factor: You could be mad for love, letting your idealized notions of Mr/Ms Perfect take over from tedious old reality. You could profitably look into your dream lover — are you punishing the one who loves you because of unrequited love for a figment?

### SCORPIO

Sun in Libra — Eros in Scorpio: this fascinating scenario can see lovely Libran You occasionally appalled by the over-the-top antics of your Eros in Scorpio. Scorp, you understand, is the sign of sex and the occult. In love, you suddenly switch on Scorp style and come across far more intensely than your Libran self can stand. The part of you that's Scorpy likes confrontational conversations that take the participants to a new level of understanding. Libra likes to amuse, flirt and cajole.

What to do: Bedwork de-angsts in a hurry.

### SAGITTARIUS

As a Sun sign Libran, you are the mistress of metaphor, the master of euphemism. You prefer your facts polished, the airbrushed look in favour of au naturel. So, what happens the moment love gets involved? You start being all gauche and candid! Why? How? Blame your Eros in Sagittarius, the sign of utter honesty. Eros in Saggo needs complete candour in all relationships, but especially love. It so irks the Libran 'dim all the lights' aspect of yourself.

Astro cliché: You're not like the others. No, really!

## CAPRICORN

Both Libra and Capricorn are extremely status conscious and aesthetically driven signs. So, you're especially about image as well as ambition. You're also a natural-born entrepreneur as both your Eros and Sun are in so-called Cardinal signs. Whatever you're involved in, you wind up in charge of the whole venture. Your Eros in Capricorn is that part of you that needs to impress and be impressed before your heart can become engaged. On its own, Libra can go for charm and cuteness. Eros in Capricorn holds out for the 'good catch'.

## AQUARIUS

Libra is the socialite, the crowd-pleaser. Aquarius is the iconoclastic maverick. Your Libran Sun is so adept at love and relationships. Eros in Aquarius isn't even sure it believes in romance. What if it's just a social construct designed to ensure mass compliance? Or something? So how come you can't stand not being in a close, simpering one-on-one relationship? Yes, if you confuse yourself, how on earth do you think you come across to others?

Astro to do: Bodywork, physicality and sensuality solve quite a lot of mental dilemmas.

## PISCES

You're the sensualist, the dreamer, the Bohemian. You're so alluring that you need to take precautions against having too many people floating around. Some kind of anti-suitor spray? Your sex appeal is ethereal and inconsistent. Both your Sun sign of Libra and your Piscean Eros are utterly changeable. You like him, you hate him but, then again, maybe not. It helps if you get to grips with your essential weirding early on. You need someone quite strong to be able to cope with your surrealism.

Astro flash: Artiste?

# Or your Psyche is in...

### ARIES

As a Sun sign Libran you're supposed to be harmonious and peace loving. But let's get one thing straight: your Psyche in Aries craves a good scrap. You're far more competitive and hyped than you may be letting on. Sports and martial arts are a wonderful way to express your Psyche sign. If this energy is not channelled healthily, it can turn into random spite or restless ambiguity.

Cosmic flash: It's lucky for you to be a 'woman's woman'. Or a man who understands them. Never reject the female side.

### TAURUS

So your Sun sign (Libra) and your Psyche sign (Taurus) are both ruled by Venus. You're attractive and aesthetically gifted. No doubt chez you is a haven of beauty and tranquillity. You're sweet and sought after. But, guess what? Beneath all that niceness lurks a tyrant! For this combo to bring you happiness, you need to make constant little adjustments to expectations. Relying overly on your winsome ways to score needs ultimately disappoints.

### GEMINI

Astro flash: Accept right now that you're so-o-o fickle! Or, as we prefer to put it, flexible and free thinking. With Sun in Libra and Psyche in Gemini, your spirit is modern. You don't like being limited by anything or anybody. You need total liberation. You may attract people who want to dominate your mind and push their (prejudiced?) point of view but that's just your little karmic challenge. They're not meant for you. Your soulmate is someone so much like you! Perhaps they even come across like a twin.

## CANCER

Libra will be ruthless about getting rid of anyone or anything she/he does not think is appropriate. For example, that daggy sofa and who cares if it's a family heirloom? Or the friend who's gone a bit 'off' of late. But Psyche in Cancer represents another aspect of you: you're also a sentimentalist. You need time and space to wallow in emotion, to be maudlin about Cousin Thing or to trawl through old love letters, mooning about the one who got away.

To do: Don't freak out at this part of yourself. Go with it. Just do it in chic Libran style!

## LEO

With Psyche in Leo, part of you definitely needs to perform. Your Sun in Libra may be able to turn over his/her share of the limelight to another but your Leonine aspect simply can't. You are naturally charismatic and able to bedazzle.

Astro weirding: No matter what the temptation you must never forsake your friends for the lover. To get in touch with your Psyche sign you could try acting, painting, dancing, singing, writing children's stories and/or just dressing up and theatrically enjoying life. Camp it up!

## VIRGO

Psyche in Virgo need not be the 'skeleton in the closet' of your gorgeous Libran house. But it can sure feel like it from time to time. As a Sun sign Libra you are above petty morality and stupid judgments. You're elegant, self-assured and cosmopolitan in outlook. But your Virgoan Psyche leaps up at the oddest times to bug you with nitpicking little concerns. You suddenly wonder whether you are shallow ... or decadent? It's Psyche in Virgo that gives you your discrimination and observational skills. Channel it via compulsive cleaning and beautifying.

# Soulmating

### LIBRA

Sun and Psyche in Libra make you a beguiling creature. You are also inclined toward harmony and must avoid those psychodramatic on-off-on-again love affairs at all costs.

Astro destiny: If other factors in your horoscope do not contradict, you are fated for one major soulmate whom you will probably meet early in life. You need peace in love. Don't let other types of people convince you otherwise. When you're feeling out of sorts, honour your Psyche sign via various forms of physical alignment, such as yoga or Pilates.

### SCORPIO

Your Sun in Libra likes the light touch. You don't like being bogged down with anything too heavy or intense. But, ha ha! You've got Psyche in Scorpio creating an emotional need for full-on relating. You really want to go there in conversations and intimate encounters, brassing off your Libran self immensely.

What to do: You are probably smart enough to gradually create your social circle of friends so that it is full of people who are similar to yourself. That way you get depth but without any horrid coarseness of perception.

### SAGITTARIUS

Psyche in Saggo needs space and lots of it. This part of you would cheerfully leap on a mystery destination flight, go extreme camping or hang out on one of those solo-in-the-wilderness kind of journeys. However, your Libran Sun thinks not. That's the version of you that loves luxury and enjoys entertaining like-minded people. But, true happiness really comes from honouring your Psyche sign and so you ideally find some way to express your inner adventurer/ adventuress...

Cosmic flash: Your soulmate could be wanderlusty or foreign.

## CAPRICORN

My dear! This can be a tough combination! Vow now to stop being so hard on yourself. Yes, you tend to carp at yourself, applying those ludicrously high standards and feeling sad when you (and nearly everyone else) falls short. For astro reasons too complicated to go into here, any angst of yours is actually best healed via you feathering your nest. Home as a true expression of your creativity becomes a source of comfort. You are also blessed with extrasensory powers of aesthetic style and harmony.
Astro flash: Style heals.

## AQUARIUS

Psyche in Aquarius is the most provocative of all. Feeling free to express your maverick leanings is a prerequisite for you feeling comfortable in the world. Yet your Sun in Libra wants only peace and concord. You officially would never say anything to offend so you are naturally confused when you come out with the oddest statement. Blame your Psyche sign and remember that you can avoid such sudden manifestations by channelling it into keeping a journal, getting involved in politics, eco issues or taking up philosophy. Accept that you're so-o-o complicated!

## PISCES

Melodramatic? You? Well, maybe just a little bit. You do, after all, have needs — and requirements. There is a little touch of the 19th century grand diva in you. Like them, you are keen on cultivating your talents and perceptions. You believe in 'singing for your supper' – that is, being always amusing and giving in a social sense. You could even change clothes 10 times a day and prefer to stay up late and sleep until noon. You are a huge believer in true romance and heaven help the person who comes between you and your illusions.

# If you are a Scorpio...
## October 24 to November 22

'Oh Lord, give me chastity and continence but not yet' prayed the Scorpio Saint Augustine in classic Scorpy mode. Your astro motto is 'I desire' and you certainly do. You're governed by Pluto, the planet of transformation. Your symbol is the Scorpion but it could just as easily be the perpetually reborn phoenix bird. You're sexy, strong and inscrutable. You make fabulous friends but the most foul enemies of all. Yes, you can be a tad obsessive and grudge-bearing. You are most renowned for your intensity. You don't take anything casually. You agree with the Scorpio military man General George S Patton who said, 'Do your damndest in an ostentatious manner all the time.'

# and your Eros is in...

# How your Sun sign gets it on with Eros & Psyche

## ARIES

Great! You like to come across as some kind of stealth bomber of love. On one hand, you're all Scorpy-smouldering sexuality and into weird — apparently never to be answered — questions and then there's your Eros in Scorpio, who is a kind of Don Quixote of love. This part of you gallops around tilting at windmills, completely freaking out the locals. You can blame your Eros in Aries for those sudden gauche announcements you make when you're in 'courtship' mode. But, you know what? You also have your Aries side to thank for your childlike belief in the power of love.

## TAURUS

Scorpio (your Sun) and Taurus (your Eros) are astro opposites. Not that you'd care. But it does create within you a kind of dynamic tension which adds to your charisma (good) and to your stress levels (not so good). Your Scorpio Sun gives you a need to look beneath the surface, to understand the workings of almost everything. You're a metaphysical kind of a person. But, Eros in Taurus projects in a far more straightforward manner and you could attract people who are not your kind at all.
To do: Tweak your public persona.

## GEMINI

Sun in Scorpio with Eros in Gemini? You must surely have chosen this set-up — in one of those karmic deals we all apparently strike — in order to teach yourself some important lesson. But what? Your Sun in Scorpio makes you a mysterious and secretive person. You like to be inscrutable. It takes years to get to know you. Eros in Gemini is out there. It's the part of you that will say anything, just for effect. Scorp is deep. Gemini is shallow. Your first romantic challenge is to better bond with yourself.
Astro flash: Love is more of a buzz when you can lighten up.

### CANCER

Scorpio and Cancer are both of the Water element, two of the most compatible signs of all. This means, happily, that there is little conflict between your core persona and the you activated when in love, or lust. You are so adept with emotions — perceiving them, feeling them, expressing them — that you could scare off the less emotionally intelligent. You ideally learn how to gauge where another is at. That is, you become more strategic (but not manipulative) with your feelings.

Astro flash: Two philosophers in love.

### LEO

You transfix people! That sexy Scorpionic gaze. The regal Leo presence. Do you even have to do anything to attract people? Or do you just sit there spider-like and wait for your 'prey' to meander into your web? This is a fascinating combo.

The potential ick factor: You could be overly keen to impress people and perhaps omit the bit where you ask about them? If the ego is in cruise control, you're a loyal and devoted lover.

Cosmic love flash: Image is a spiritual issue to you, not a matter of political correctness.

### VIRGO

Left to your own devices, you can be a bit taciturn. Your desire to project mystery may actually manifest as someone who seems to be a bit glum. That's the Sun in Scorpio for you. So thank heavens for your Virgoan Eros, the storyteller, gossip and info-broker of the Zodiac. This side of you prefers to seduce via mental communion. It's a useful antidote to the Scorpy silent treatment. But the 'Scorpio with feeling' side of you serves to deepen the sometimes overly rational Virgo Eros.

In love: You love the mutual 'shrinking' style of relationship.

# LIBRA

Scorpio wants intense rapport. Your idea of a fun conversation is drilling right down to the important stuff. For example, the new world order and saving the planet. Libra likes to cajole and charm. In love, you go a bit Libran and project as light-hearted, gloriously shallow and perhaps even slightly faux. Then, as someone gets to know the 'real you', they get blasted with the full force of Scorpionic passion, paranoia and conspiracy theories.

Astro ick potential: Don't succumb to any hermit urges. Love really *is* like oxygen to you.

# SCORPIO

Sun and Eros in Scorpio? You could be like something out of a silent movie, all goobly eyes, Cupid-bowed lips and yearning writhing. With this combination you probably only have two speeds in relationships. You either don't give a damn — in which case you can't be bothered even registering a person's presence on earth. The other reaction is that you are extraordinarily in love, realizing that this is one of the most significant relationships of your life, if not *the* one.

Astro resolution: Don't even bother pretending to have casual dalliances. They won't work.

# SAGITTARIUS

For reasons you may not fully understand — yet — you can project a completely different persona in romance. Imagine this. Here you are, a sexy and deep-thinking Scorpio, and yet one hint of lust, love or even like and you turn all Saggo, vibing sporty, light-hearted and generally gung-ho. You could find yourself gabbing away at a million miles an hour, making faux pas all over the place, eagerly nodding 'yes' to spontaneous away trips when normally you like to thoroughly investigate the terrain or person. It's Eros in Sagg. It's you, too!

# Soulmating

## CAPRICORN

So how come so many of your romance scenarios resemble daytime television drama? You're possibly a super control-freak! Chic (or suave), empowered with a brilliant career and determined never to show a single shred of weakness. Both your Sun and Eros signs are intense and obsessed with relationship real politik. Luckily, you scare off all but your true psycho peers, your twin souls who want to enjoy a spot of power-struggling with you. Astro hint: Never get involved with someone weaker or overly needy. They'll wind up running you!

## AQUARIUS

As a Sun sign Scorpio, you're very deep and obsessed with meaning and perhaps a little overly interested in conspiracy theories. And your Eros in Aquarius is surprisingly similar! Yet there is one major difference. Aquarius shies away from intimacy. Scorpio needs to sense it for the conversation to even get going. You have myriad 'tests' that you run before allowing rapport to boot up. So, once you're attracted to someone, your Eros takes over and creates an impression of you that is quite different to your wildly emotive Scorp self.

## PISCES

Your combination of Eros in Pisces and Sun in Scorpio reels in would-be lovers like nothing else on this planet. It's like you can zoom into someone else's mind and say what needs to be said for maximum impact. You're fabulous at creating instant intimacy. People meet you for just five minutes and already you've got your own little 'us' jokes going. And, of course, you are horrendously attractive. The Eros in Pisces adds a lighter touch to your famed Scorpy intensity.
Potential ick factor: You giving off falsely flirty signals.

# Or your Psyche is in...

## ARIES

Your Sun in Scorpio is so subtle and cunning. Your Psyche in Aries is anything but! Remembering that we should honour our Psyche sign for psychological wellbeing, what are you supposed to do? Kickboxing? Netball? Debating? Synchronized swimming? Karaoke competitions? Yes, that's right. All or any of the above will do to give your Arean Psyche a healthy outlet. If not? You seethe away, becoming competitive in inappropriate situations of intimacy.

## TAURUS

Scorpio and Taurus are opposite signs of the Zodiac so going with your Psyche in Taurus will make you feel more balanced and real. It will actually enhance your Scorpionic Sun. You have an aspect of yourself that is simple where your Scorpy self is complex. You ideally learn to relax and realize that some scenarios do, in fact, have *très* obvious solutions. As Taurus is the sign of the Earth Angel, you will find any form of gardening (don't roll your eyes) to be cathartic, thought-provoking and relaxing.

## GEMINI

Your Scorpio Sun is Fixed. Psyche in Gemini is Mutable. The Sun in Scorpio likes to drill down deep into any issue. Glib Gemini gleans just as much meaning from skimming across the surface. It is as if you need to send constant memos between these disparate parts of yourself. But the effort is so worth it. Your Psyche in Gemini needs the anchoring effects of your Sun sign but your Scorpio aspects so benefit from the no-hassle insights of the Psyche. Vow now: Have whole days when you just dabble.

# Soulmating

## CANCER

Your Sun and Psyche signs are so compatible. You must surely find it fairly easy to gain peace and clarity.

Astro destiny: Maybe you feel bizarrely drawn to another country? As a child, did you experience a special connection to another place or its people? You are hugely likely to be psychic and your feelings about where others are at will aid you and them. But this may certainly hinder your love life as you doubt your sensitivity — and even beauty! — and find yourself drawn to lovers who will make it go underground.

## LEO

As a Scorpio, you are naturally shy and a creature of mystery. You can take years to reveal some hidden talent of yours — or that you once had your own television show or whatever. It's part of that Scorpio mystique. But with your Psyche in performance-artiste Leo, the game is up! You need to be more of a luvvie for your own psycho wellbeing. It's astro prescribed. Getting over your inhibitions in this regard will enhance every aspect of your life. Which talent have you been nurturing in secret? What skill have you been ignoring or refusing to talk about? It's time!

## VIRGO

Believe it or not, your combination of Sun and Psyche signs finds bliss via massive household-filth purges. You're successful at whatever you set your mind to — corporate sharkery, surfing, global enterprise — but for true fulfilment, cleaning, administrivia and general Tao of organizing activities are the go for you. What to beware of? Nitpicking and guilting. You could be far too prone to holding a grudge.

Astro destiny flash: Quite apart from romantic love, a close friend is likely to be a special soulmate of yours.

## LIBRA

Your Sun in Scorpio often likes to see itself as ruggedly individualist. Deep down, you don't need anybody, let alone their stupid opinion. So it can be difficult for you to assimilate your Psyche in Libra. This is an astro energy that truly cares about what other people think and likes to be surrounded by them, well, always. And expressing your Psyche is vital for holistic fabulosity.

Think it through: Isn't it true that there's always been an aspect of you who's a person who needs people? Opening up to others can be an amazingly rewarding experience for you.

## SCORPIO

With both your Sun and Psyche in Scorpio, you probably have a decent understanding of yourself and your motivations. You would also be highly tuned in to the not-so-secret (to you, anyway) thoughts of other people. From an early age you realize that you can't just switch off this flow of insights.

Your big astro challenge: To learn how to separate the incoming (other people's stuff) from your own emotions and ideas. Astro flash: Don't allow less profound types to talk you into disowning your truth.

## SAGITTARIUS

As a Sun sign Scorpio, you could be slightly irked by your Psyche in Sagg. You are strategic and are able to hold back the gush of conversation in order to get what you want. However, the Psyche-in-Sagg side of you just says 'whatever'. Yes, there is an important part of you that needs to be able to say whatever you feel like, however you feel like it and whenever it works for you, without having to process the emotion behind it or think through whether or not it's appropriate.

Astro karma drama: Learning to love your inner 'galah'.

# Soulmating

### CAPRICORN

You're the It Person of whatever your scene is but, boy, do you know how to burn out your brain cells with over-achievement. Scorpio is, of course, the sign of compulsive-obsessive ambition and so is Capricorn! It's great should you be trying to put in untold slog to achieve some awesome, rarely attained end — that is, beating the world record for shot-put — but tricky when it comes to relaxing and going to sleep at night. Or maybe you don't? Psyche in Cap can find staying up all night to brainstorm brilliant career schemes more relaxing.

### AQUARIUS

Both Scorpio and Aquarius are so-called Fixed signs. You can find it so easy to become stuck in one attitude or persona. Yet your Aquarian Psyche finds peace and harmony via looking into ideas that challenge you. You can always heal angst by investigating a whole new tangent of thought. This is often the combo of the beautiful loner — no matter how crowded your life, part of you feels essentially alone. In love, you tend to extremes. You're either single for seemingly ever or happily married at a *très* young age. It's like there is Scorpy You — the last of the red-hot lovers, even if it is just in your lunchtime and the Ice Maiden within.

### PISCES

Psyche in Pisces is the Prince/Princess position, a nice blend with your Scorpio Sun. As a double Water sign, you are powerfully intuitive and creative. Love often follows from some creative endeavour of yours or, weirder, via another lover! Psyche in Pisces requires that you take frequent little mental breaks, swimming away from the usual haunts so that you can tune in to other realities. Of all people, you are the most aware that there are weirder forces in the world than we imagine.

# If you are a Sagittarius...
## November 23 to December 21

Spunky, fun-loving and incorrigibly candid, you can also be self-centred and irresponsible. You're renowned for 'foot in mouth' disease, often leaving behind a wake of people gasping 'Did she say that?' You are also the great escape artiste of the Zodiac, a traveller and adventurer through life. This can also have its drawbacks. Like Saggo cartoon genius Charles Schultz, you think that 'no problem is so formidable that you can't walk away from it.' In love you demand — and dish out in return — an exceptional combo of space and loyalty. Your ultimate Saggo advice for life comes from British playwright Noël Coward who said: 'You've got to look after your legend.'

# and your Eros is in...

# Soulmating

### ARIES

Easy-peasy! Sagittarius and Aries are probably the two most similar signs of all! Both are gregarious, extroverted and non-interested in tedium no matter what the societal rewards. Some call it tactlessness but both signs are also proud of telling it like it is. So your Eros in Aries enhances your Sun in Sagittarius, making you even more charismatic (and bombastic) than you already are. Yes, you are a double Fire sign with the sunny persona and the heat to prove it.

Astro flash: The art of listening may be your greatest achievement.

### TAURUS

Astro destiny: Work and wellbeing somehow play an interesting role in your love life! You meet your soulmate on the day job? At the gym? Wait and see. Okay so you are a Sun sign Sagittarius, totally into freedom for yourself and everyone else. What of this Eros in Taurus? It means you could come across in love quite unlike the way you truly are. Partners get a hell of a fright when you suddenly announce — in typical Sagg style — that you've thrown in the stupid job and are heading off to South America to be a tennis coach for a year.

### GEMINI

Gemini and Sagittarius are opposite signs of the Zodiac. Your Eros in Gemini makes you even more fascinating than the 'typical' Saggo! You're charming and entertaining, possibly the ultimate raconteur. So why do you wind up somehow psychologically tormenting so many would-be adorees? The Gemini You is prone to telling a few little white lies. It's just for entertainment's sake, you understand. However, this is totally at odds with your core — and so candid — Sagg personality.

Cosmic flash: You are the ultimate requirer of space.

## CANCER

Sun in Sagittarius and Eros in Cancer! You're an odd bird all right but nobody cares because you're so quirky and cute. The Sun in Saggo, as you know, is all about speed, cheek and freedom. You've got a personality that's a bit like that of the Road Runner too. However, your Eros in Cancer means you get one whiff of love and, suddenly, you come over all emotional! Your feelings flow. The one thing you and your Eros have in common is that both Sagg and Cancer are honest signs ... but you just can't bear how clingy you become in relationships. Accept it ASAP.

## LEO

You're a glamour queen/king! Your Saggo Sun combines brilliantly with this Eros in Leo to produce a proud, gorgeous and fun-loving monster of ego. In love, you go all out to impress, and you do! Nobody is as full on as you on your day ... or night.

The potential ick factor: You may not know how to listen to another person. You could get so wound up in your performance that you don't notice the 'audience' quietly snoozing off behind that dutifully attentive air.

Vow now: To work on this. Give back to your fan club.

## VIRGO

Eros in Virgo is the seducer via detail. For example, 'I love that tie', 'I really admire what you did today in the boardroom', and so on. Nothing escapes the goobly bedroom eyes of Eros in Virgo. Okay, so what happens when your Saggo self — the big picture, don't bother with the minutiae, it's the forest, not the trees — emerges? You so often have this interesting romance destiny of meeting your partners literally on the job. Eros in Virgo can even insist on employing his/her former lovers which brings with it all kinds of interesting complications.

# Soulmating

### LIBRA

Your ideal love persona is that of best friends doing everything exciting together. You have this blissful idealized-companion thing going on in your mind. Sagittarius loves the idea of a buddy for life with sex thrown in and your Eros in Libra is the most likely Eros of all to want pair-bonding. Yet you can freak out at the slightest hint of dissent. For all your talk about honesty, you can't hack authentic emotional expression.

Astro flash: One person — your true lover — arrives for extended education on the issue du jour.

### SCORPIO

Does your Eros in Scorpio wanna write a cheque that your Sun in Sagittarius can't cash? Your Eros sign adds a deeper dimension to your beautiful Saggo persona and certainly a sexier vibe. You are more sensitive and emotionally aware than the 'average' Sagittarius. And yet you could inadvertently lead people on by being so intense and also, ultimately, because you are a Sagittarius, the relationship you want is less fraught, more fun and companionable. You make Water signs (Pisces, Cancerians, Scorpios) go really gaga.

### SAGITTARIUS

Okay, so you win some kind of award for honesty in love. You can't help but be authentic. With Eros and the Sun in Sagittarius, nobody is going to be in a moment's doubt about where they stand with you. Your seduction style is more of a non-stop monologue rant, complete with an inbuilt CV and a summary of the latest jokes. Amazingly, you can pull in the prospective partners. Cosmic love lesson: To slow it down, take a deep breath and tune into what other people are trying to tell you.

Astro cliché: You can run and hide.

## CAPRICORN

As a Sagittarius you are feck-free and liberated. You certainly don't give a crap for pompous drivel and other people's ideas of what constitutes a good life. Respectability? Whatever. You make up your own rules. But with Eros in Capricorn, part of you is seriously turned on by success and even power-mongering. You do get more interested in people if you think they've got it together in the material-security stakes and you're not totally unmoved by the idea of having piles of money. Can you be an honest enough Sagg enough to admit this aspect of your character?

## AQUARIUS

Sun in Sagittarius and Eros in Aquarius? You are utterly without artifice. Your sweet authenticity disarms even the most game-playing of would-be lovers. But that's not to say that you are not complicated. You just prefer to deal with it yourself, rather than foisting it onto others. Humour is one of your many saving graces, along with a catch-me-if-you-can and hard-to-get kind of appeal. You're so naturally independent and amazing that you never have to play any idiot games. Look out for those psychic vampires, who try to drain your independence.

## PISCES

Welcome to the Wilding! You're untamable, completely alluring – the sexy beast of civilized romance. You are so easily bored that, if you are to find long-term love, you essentially need someone as changeable and practically feral as you. You're a surrealist and a big schemer. You are immensely candid in some areas (only when it suits you) and an amazingly good fibber in others – once again, only when it suits you. Nobody leaves behind a bigger selection of broken hearts than you but, somehow, you turn the whole thing around to you being the victim.

# Or your Psyche is in...

### ARIES

All you want is a room of your own. Or maybe an island of your own. It'll need lots of space for you and your ego. You believe in true romance but only with the person you consider good enough to mate with the Great You. This paragon may take time to find but that won't stop you practising on lesser beings in the meantime. The challenge: You find spiritual peace through ranting on about yourself but who will listen? Money, beauty and/or being good in bed help your romantic cause immensely.

### TAURUS

Psyche in Taurus blends nicely with your Sun in Sagittarius. Both signs are nature lovers though Taurus can prefer the wilderness slightly more manicured than does the Saggo side of you. You find your tranquillity and heart's ease by being close to the green, and also by slowing down the Saggo speed-racer mentality and embracing the Taurean sloth ethos. You realize there is nothing wrong with a night (a week?) spent on the couch. Ditto, you enter the comfort zone via gourmet foodie experiences. So non-Sagg.

### GEMINI

Your Saggo Sun likes to make big statements about everything. But the wellbeing of your Psyche relies on bolstering your soapbox pedestal experience with Gemini-style trivia, apparently useless facts and gossip. Whenever you are feeling down, the gleaning and brokering of info will always feel healing. In relationships, a talk about something seemingly inconsequential often works better for you than the big official 'us' chat.

## CANCER

Astro destiny: It's amazing how a seemingly tedious obligation, something to do with debt or in-laws or a former lover, will bring you closer to a profound and significant life scenario. But this combination is also about owning up to deeper emotional realities beneath the Saggo bluster. Your famed candour should extend beyond tactlessness and into admitting a few feelings. With your Cancerian Psyche you find that the sharing (that's as in you and someone else relating, not just you banging on to a not-so-rapt audience) can be just so healing.

## LEO

Your Sun in Sagittarius is an adventurer/adventuress. You may dislike staying in one place for too long and sometimes you even have issues about creating a permanent home base for yourself. However, Psyche in Leo demands a firm centre for genius to best flourish. Yes, genius. This Psyche sign is all about the nurturing and developing of your talent. Psychic peace comes through this process, whether it be stand-up comedy, writing stories for children or photography. You can't run away from it.

## VIRGO

Psyche in Virgo is that insistent little inner voice of the nagging cavalier saying, 'Sagittarius You, have you taken your vitamins, today? Do you really want to take this trip instead of paying your credit card by the due date? Isn't that outfit too young for you?' Eeek! But this Psyche sign provides a valuable brake for some of your more extreme Saggo 'path of excess leads to the palace of wisdom' moments. You're more discriminating, employable and (yes!) classy than the 'average' Saggo. Owning up to control-freaky tendencies makes Pysche in Virgo more appealing.
Astro flash: You're in denial about being fusspotty in love.

### LIBRA

You believe fully in free love but you want the one you love to be by your side, all the time ... except for when you suddenly need space that second and your partner is expected to vacate the premises, leaving you with all his/her money, of course. Psyche in Libra can be easily evoked and pampered via aesthetic surroundings (unlike many a Sagg, who are spiritually allergic to tackiness) and the day spa reality.

Astro challenge: To learn how to afford others the same privileges you so sweetly demand for yourself.

### SCORPIO

The combination of Sun in Sagittarius and Psyche in Scorpio? You're highly sexed and mega-spiritual! No way are you going to give up either aspect of yourself — for example, by becoming a celibate yoga guru — because you are also someone who crusades on the having-it-all cause. You are a fascinating blend of extroverted blunder-puss and mysterious traveller through life. Always remember that Psyche in Scorpio needs to be acknowledged. You are naturally drawn to studies in psychology, the occult and religion.

### SAGITTARIUS

Restless and ambiguous about every aspect of your life, you aim to be forever evolving. Both your Sun and Psyche in Saggo need fresh air, new horizons and the freedom to change your mind whenever you feel like it. In love? You seek someone who will let you be you, even if you being you does involve a cast of hundreds — friends, other lovers, travelling companions, your osteopath — and, guess what? Such a person is almost impossible to find.

To avoid: Hooking up with someone who is inferior and then making their life a misery.

## CAPRICORN

Your Psyche in Capricorn makes you a lot more security-conscious than the classic Sagittarius! You have a higher chance of being able to fund all your Saggo navel-gazing, sports activities and travel. You have the enviable knack of fitting into systems and then subtly subverting the paradigm so that you get precisely what you want. Mediocrities loathe you. They watch you strutting out of the office early to go surfing or for a ski weekend. You have your work all done, the client is in love with you and wonder, how you do it! Not even you know!

## AQUARIUS

Both your Sagittarius Sun and Psyche in Aquarius can have a few issues with intimacy. It's not that you can't fake it if you need to but your base attitude is along the lines of 'Why bother?' However, you tend to attract high-maintenance lovers with intense demands for reassurance and closeness.

What to do: You ideally recognize that these people (they will quite often be Water signs — Cancer, Pisces, Scorpio) are drawn to you for a spiritual reason. Yes, they're there to ensure that you actually get a life and have a heart.

## PISCES

Astro challenge: Psyche in Pisces means you need to go against Saggo wanderlusty instincts and create a beautiful base camp situation for yourself. Nest-feathering will always make you happy at heart. This is an amazing blend of two individualista signs. You're utterly original and unable to be tamed. Yet, like some strange wild unicorn creature, you allow yourself to be a doting idiot for love with just a few people. Others can ask you the time and you hit the roof about commitment, encroachments upon your precious privacy, etc.

# If you are a Capricorn...
## September 24 to October 23

You're sophisticated, loyal and know how to commit to someone. In love — as in business — there is no fickleness in the Goat. You're a highly focused, upwardly mobile person who sees mating activity in similar terms. From the outside, you can seem rigid, suited to corporations and government. But in your relationships, your sign often attracts someone very different to you: it is not unusual for the Goat lawyer to marry the artist or the writer. Your greatest assets? A physiognomy that defies age: you look younger as you get older. But, above all, Caps lure lovers with their get-ahead personalities. Or, as Capricorn billionaire Howard Hughes put it, 'success is the best deodorant'.

# and your Eros is in...

# How your Sun sign gets it on with Eros & Psyche

## ARIES

Fire and ice? When a Capricorn has Eros in Aries, it is either the bane of their life or their saving grace. Capricorn is symbolized by the Goat — tenacious, loyal and solid as a rock. Nothing gets between them and their precious status, which can make them seem cold. This personality is turned on its head when their love nature is ruled by Eros in Aries. This is a fiery, passionate and physically driven energy. It's impulsive and hair-triggered and can lead Capricorn into many regrettable couplings. The ideal way to handle this? Keep your loving in the bedroom and your money in the bank. In other words, allow Aries to rule your Eros but quarantine that mad-dash energy from your fiscal energy.

## TAURUS

Love out of focus? For the highly driven Capricorn, having Eros in Taurus is likely to feel confusing. The Goat is about scaling the mountain — it's about endeavour, and the love nature follows this. But the Cow is a grazer of lush pastures and an enjoyer of effortless rounds of seduction, sex and romance. Eros in Taurus means you're a natural and potential lovers feel this very strongly about the Taurean energy. For Caps it could be a fillip if they can just unbutton a little and go with it.

## GEMINI

Capricorns may like to put a bit of effort into thinking how to handle their love nature. Their Sun sign is organized, trustworthy and a person who can be relied upon to follow through on promises. But their love lives may clash with this if they have Eros in Gemini. Not to put it too daintily, the Eros in Gem energy can be heavily themed in favour of fibs, fickleness and flirting. Gems love the sparkle and the laughter — getting them to an altar may trigger issues. Worth thinking this over.

## CANCER

Capricorns with Eros in Cancer may have the perfect approach to their relationships. On an outward level, the Goat Person is reliable, ambitious and loyal. But adding this to the Eros in Cancer energy brings a whole new dimension of nurturing and empathy into the relationship. It is a wonderful mixture that balances the Capricorn drive for success with an instinctive sense of how to love and how to parent. It means you can be hard in the boardroom and soft in the home. The only drawback? Eros in Cancer comes with a walloping great temper.

## LEO

What do you get when you cross a corporate Titan-in-training with someone whose falling-in-love extravaganzas come with great flourishes of flowers and grandiose announcements? Try a Capricorn Sun sign with Eros in Leo. When Eros in Leo rules the love nature of the pragmatic and hard-headed Capricorn, two personalities have to essentially live side by side. Can the über-Caps make luvvie phone calls from an all-important meeting? With Eros in Leo, they will certainly give it a try.
Astro flash: Power-tripping in relationships.

## VIRGO

A match made in seventh heaven? Capricorns with Eros in Virgo have a love nature that fits almost perfectly. Eros in Virgo is about sophistication, pickiness and discernment. They are just like canny Capricorns. The big difference in the Virgo love nature is the comparative worldliness about sex and romance matters — subjects that many Goats have not stopped to dwell upon.
Astro karma drama: You tend to fall in love with highly strung, mega-emotional types who then proceed to cast you as the relationship's official police officer.

## LIBRA

So fussy! You vibe like one of those spoiled pedigree show cats. Capricornian elegance and standards are fine when it comes to business outcomes, yet it's hard to carry these benchmarks over into your love life. No matter, as Eros in Libra is the all-time relationship guru. From a very early age, you've been studying the labyrinths of love and sex. As a result, you give the best advice in the Zodiac. You are, okay, amazingly 'looksist' and manipulative. The loving space is your domain and you can't resist opportunities to swing things your way with a few passive-aggressive ploys. Astro flash: You have a psychic sense of smell. It's true!

## SCORPIO

Capricorn with Eros in Scorpio would do well to watch for any personality crisis that might threaten with the combination of these two so-powerful signs. This mix has the capacity to produce a sexually magnetic person who is focused in love and who does not tell lies. However, the result could also be rigidity, paranoia, inappropriate intensity and a focus on the negative rather than the positive. Watch for an internal clash between the Eros-in-Scorpio's interest in the soul and your Goaty material obsession.

## SAGITTARIUS

Solid as a rock ... but about to fly away? So goes the dilemma when a Capricorn has Eros in Sagittarius. Capricorn, the Goat, is sure-footed but constantly upwardly mobile. You are a real rock, a reliable player of systems and all the trappings of the good egg. However, give the Goat the love nature informed by Eros in Sagittarius and you have some interesting results. The solid citizen act may hide a flighty heart of passion. For example, you would be prepared to drop everything if it meant pursuing love's freedom of the heart!

## CAPRICORN

Hint: Vow now not to write up a template document binding your potential lover to minimal hours of work at a certain level of salary. With Eros in Capricorn, the Goat could easily slide into a rigid system of relationship management where the objects of their interest are put through the money-status-sanity test every day. The Capricorn interest in the material world is understandable but constantly talking in terms of pre-nuptial agreements and rights waivers is not really a love life. Is it?

## AQUARIUS

Even the straightest Capricorns, with the most stable employment histories, could find themselves heavily involved with an anarcho-communist or an experimental refugee poet thanks to Eros in Aquarius. This Aquarian influence is an explorer of people rather than the Goaty judger. The Eros-in-Aquarius love life is therefore total anathema to the Capricorn personality. Caps think that people who are too interesting may be a liability while Eros in Aqua will not touch anyone who is not interesting *enough*! When you put these factors together in a love nature, the results could be either very happy or quite disastrous.

## PISCES

Canny Cap in the kaftan? Capricorns may spend all day doing banking deals or making money for people, but when they have Eros in Pisces they have love lives that are quite obviously out there. Eros in Pisces translates as highly emotional, instinctive and in contact with universal themes such as love, sex and power. The Eros-in-Pisces love nature is difficult, temperamental and highly artistic. Where, exactly, it can be integrated with the Capricorn love of order is the challenge.

Astro bonus: People can't help but be intrigued.

# Or your Psyche is in...

## ARIES

Lacking energy? Listless? No motivation? It sounds like advertising for a new vitamin supplement but in terms of your love life it could be as simple as accessing your secret Ram. With Psyche in Aries, Capricorns are given the secret key to a love nature they may have wished they had. With this Psyche energy, a Cap with the right motives can evolve beyond their outward personality and trigger a far more dynamic and risk-taking love persona.

Astro hint: Access the energy but not the craziness.

## TAURUS

You have the shares portfolio, the corner office and the flash house. But is something missing? Some Caps get too rigid about themselves and try to run a relationship in the same way they run an investment strategy. If you have Psyche in Taurus you are in a very good position to tune in to a sensual side of yourself and lose some rigidity. The Taurean influence is at the adequate end of the love and sex spectrum. Tune in, work at it and it all falls into place.

## GEMINI

An irresponsible imp just waiting to get out? You are all status and maturity on the surface ... and sometimes you feel that it shows in your love nature. But when Caps have Psyche in Gemini you have a reservoir of flighty and fickle behaviour itching to unleash itself. Psyche in Gemini is the energy of the love-taker and heartbreaker — without a word of malice, just a wink and a laugh. When Canny Goats learn to tap into this secret love persona, they learn how to unlock a whole new universe for themselves.

## CANCER

Time to soften your image? Ready to go into the touchy-feely space where the heart overrules the head? Capricorns with Psyche in Cancer have a secret power source that is theirs to unlock when they decide to go there. Of course, most of you spend your lives avoiding losing control or appearing too vulnerable to what lies in the heart. If you want to see how the other side of life exists in love, entrust your love nature to your Psyche-in-Cancer guide. A great balancer, if nothing else.

## LEO

Longing to try on the duck suit? Toying with a small costume or maybe an accent in the boudoir? With Psyche in Leo you *très* straight Caps could be hiding an instinct to camp it up and put on a show. Or, if you're solo at the moment, the Psyche-in-Leo energy is all about being more dramatic and diva-like. Psyche rules the secret You and accessing your inner Leo love nature requires some leaps of faith.

To do: Think creativity — try singing, go to the opera or dress up in a spangled leotard and stand at the front of your group exercise class. The typical Goat looks at a luvvie Leo and is mildly appalled at the vulgarity. But, it's true — Big Cats have more fun.

## VIRGO

When you're a Capricorn Sun sign with Psyche in Virgo it's a good indicator that there may be a more sensual you hiding beneath the serious, responsible Goat that you project to the world. Psyche rules your secret love nature and when it's in Virgo it's a very strong opportunity for you. Feeling a bit unworldly with sex or slightly not with it in the flirting and pouncing stakes? The sophistication and sensual confidence of Psyche in Virgo is a perfect surprise package to unlock and let into your armory.

## LIBRA

Are you *really* so certain? Caps can become slightly too fond of your certainties — great when you're a fund manager or senior bureaucrat, but not so hot when you're in relationships. To take the edge off your empirical approach to life and love you could make some effort to access your Psyche-in-Libra influences. Libra in love is about weighing things up and avoiding the tags of 'right' and 'wrong'. Pysche in Libra takes an easy question and turns it into a dilemma. However, Caps would simply call it dithering.

Astro flash: Psyche in Libra loves good looks and your soul could certainly do with some bubbly spa time.

## SCORPIO

What on Earth could Psyche in Scorpio bring to Capricorn? Well, one of the biggest image perceptions that you lot may like to overturn is that image of you as the person who manages a love affair in the same way you manage your wealth planning. That is, with as little emotion as possible. Tuning into the secret love nature as set out by Psyche in Scorpio allows you to admit to greater levels of intensity and everlasting love. Whether you want this or not, it is your secret love nature, so *listen* to it.

## SAGITTARIUS

There's no rule to say that Capricorns don't drink or raise hell at any time. However, you lot generally don't do it like a Sagittarius. Saggo will dance on a table, recite poems or do handstands if it means there's a good chance of it leading to a romantic conquest. When you have Psyche in Sagittarius you have a secret side to your love nature that really wants to be extroverted and loud about the pursuit of romance. It's not like this behaviour is an alien thing that is out to embarrass you. This is You.

The eeek factor: If in doubt, go out!

## CAPRICORN

Regardez! The perfectly integrated Canny Cap! When you outwardly have the ambition, the organization and the pragmatic approach to your life and you also have the secret love nature of Psyche in Capricorn, you are aligned as the cosmos may well have intended it. Your take on success and wealth-building — that it can only be done by never dealing with any tricky or mad person — is cemented when Psyche is in Capricorn. You pretend to like the duds, but Psyche brings you back to reality.

## AQUARIUS

Go on, admit it! You Capricorns can't go through your lives having romances that mirror your careers. It's lucky that you have Psyche in Aquarius — your secret love nature and the ultimate key to happiness. Many Caps would repress this influence because it skews heavily toward unorthodox people and potentially dangerous ideas. If you developed such romantic tastes, who knows where it could lead? You could even find happiness with someone that the bank doesn't approve of.

## PISCES

The Bourgeois-Bohemian romance? When you Capricorns have Psyche in Pisces, you have to think very carefully about where you want to take this. The Pisces energy is a bit like the *Cat in the Hat* and the nagging but sensible fish is the Capricorn. Goats are hardly cold — they are ruttish Earth signs after all. But the Capricorn in love is a person in control and not given to the highs and lows or the workplace 'us' chats of other types of people. Because Pisces is highly emotional, in touch with dreams, artistic and slightly unstable, you may decide that you'll have to repress this side of yourself. However, it is your secret love nature and you may gain more by accepting it than by totally rejecting it.

# If you are an Aquarius...
## January 21 to February 19

Your astro motto is 'I know'. And you really think you do. You know about the law of aerodynamics, how pollen works and how to make uranium batteries. But with love matters you can vibe cold and distant, unable or unwilling to engage in silly concepts such as monogamy and mutual trust. You are a revolutionary thinker and officially hilarious. But you also need a 'security blanket' lover at home while insisting on your 'freedom'. Not surprisingly, you have fun trying to reconcile this love nature with a serious affair. 'It's really hard to maintain a one-on-one relationship if the other person is not going to allow you to see other people'. — Guns N' Roses lead singer Axl Rose.

# and your Eros is in...

# Soulmating

## ARIES

Your usual wise-cracking, unorthodox persona sits well with the hyped-up Ram energy that is also big on joking and owning up to a totally unique personality. The Eros-in-Aries outlook is also that they are the genius and others are there to support their brilliance — a system that works fine for Aquarians. Where these influences come undone is in stickability: the Aries way is to stick with their mate through everything. Aquarians, however, need a bit of help to understand the monogamy concept.

Astro flash: Think friendship, not ownership.

## TAURUS

You have a life in the mind — Taurus has very much a life of the body. So when you theoretical and highly intelligent Aqua-Maddies with Eros in Taurus stray into the realm of love, you can surprise everyone with your readiness and expertise. Anyone who has Eros in Taurus should count themselves lucky. Taurus is ruled by Venus and the Cow's love energy is totally natural and sensual. What to do when feeling blue: Access your peaceful Taurus self via nature ... think garden, greenery, wilderness. Just being outdoors for you is very is healing.

## GEMINI

Here comes trouble! You lot are already a bit shy of the commitment side of love and even when you do settle down you like to feel that your lover is there as a sort of support act. So go figure out how irritating it could be to have your love nature ruled by the vagaries of Eros in Gemini. An Aquarius with this Eros should watch very carefully for being a lying, glib flirter who collects hearts and breaks them. It's a good idea to tune into the best of Gemini. Mix with great communicators. This includes those who are good at writing letters.

# CANCER

This is the love switcheroo: the normal insistence of most Aquarians that their lover play the at-home hearth-keeper role is reversed when Eros is in Cancer. This energy triggers your need to be the nurturer, to provide the warm place to come home to. More than any other Eros energy, this is the one that pushes Aquarians into a whole new space. It's a very female Eros indicator and it is also one that can come with a range of terrible moods.

Astro nightmare: You freaking out when your lover won't go for the special crank diet that you've just concocted.

# LEO

Taking flowers home to Mr/Mrs Aqua? Wooing the talent with romantic candlelit dinners and weekends away? Chances are you have Eros in Leo. You can be the coldest, most distant Aquarian, astral-travelling through the Cosmos of your own genius. But Eros in Leo makes you treat the pursuit of love as a big excuse to put on a grand show. All of that Aquarian insouciance seems to falls away when you start putting some real theatre back into love. Eros in Leo is the influence that comes to the fore when you're out dancing the night away or wandering through a picturesque vineyard. Whether it comes out in the pursuit of love or in the consolidation phase, it's the luvvie romantic impulses that give it away. It's the rose between the teeth and the little love poems.

To do: Learn to love your Eros in Leo; it's important, as this is what gives you your warmth and charisma.

# VIRGO

Having trouble connecting the romantic dots? This is not an unusual problem with Aquarians — you deal better with ideas and stories than you do with other people who may actually need something. However, when you have Eros in Virgo you are blessed with sophisticated romancing skills. Make all the jokes you want about control-freaky Virgos, but they sure know how to run relationships.

Astro flash: Noting something via your super-human powers of observation does not place you under any obligation whatsoever to voice it.

### LIBRA

By day, you lot could easily be real know-it-alls. You're very smart people who are paid never to have a second of a doubt about your expertise. But when you have Eros in Libra you may be blessed with some equivocation. Some people call it dithering, but the Eros-in-Libra vibe is also about being able to see both sides. The Aquarius You is a know-all. And Libra is conciliatory. The only drawback of this Eros? Libra is an absolute looks-snob. The beauty standard is very high for Lib and that clashes with your Aquarius 'love everybody equally' ethos.

### SCORPIO

Learning to live with your alter ego? The standard relationship pattern for Aquarians is to find a mate who will be happy to keep house, while the Aqua genius gets out and about. But when Eros in Scorpio is your love nature you are far more focused and intense about where your lover is and how much they love you. When your Eros is in Scorpio you break all the Aquarian rules and actually admit to jealousy. Yes, you are likely to be far more in touch with your emotions than the classic Aquarius of legend.

### SAGITTARIUS

If you Aquarians are lucky enough to have Eros in Sagittarius, you may have landed the love nature most compatible with your general outlook. Eros in Sagittarius bolsters your instincts to keep the romantic intensity at 'low' while pursuing lots of other interests. The Eros-Saggo vibe is also skewed toward theoretical love as opposed to the physical and emotional psychodrama that so many often demand.

Astro flash: You are a mixture of Fire and Air and, as such, you are both attractive and inspiring. But try not to outsource your emotions to your partner.

## CAPRICORN

The Aquarius You is appalled by your Eros in Capricorn. You are a radically minded, aware and socially progressive creature. Your Eros in Capricorn cares about societal structures. Cap does not want to tear them down as you would like to do to a few, but in order to be an actual pillar of it. Yes, it's your secret straight! But, your Eros in Capricorn is also a blessing. Cap is a sensual sign and so it antidotes some of your Aquarian live-in-the-mind frigidity. Astro flash: True teamwork and deep friendship come before lust and true love.

## AQUARIUS

If your experiences of love have no bearing on what you read in romance novels, then you could have Eros in Aquarius. With this energy, you don't get it ... and you don't care. You have a romantic model but it has nothing to do with putting your feet up with spousie and doing a bit of canoodling. You have a meeting to go to or an obsessive hobby to put time into. Yes, and it does make you happy. You relish the idea of a romance that's like no other — but it's one that liberates and intoxicates in equal measure with no demands. It's a figment!

## PISCES

What would happen if someone had all the outward signs of being a bit of a cold fish, but in the pursuit of their love life they were needy, skittish and totally subsumed with emotion? They would probably have Eros in Pisces — the love nature that throws the Aquarian coolness on the scrap heap and delivers instead a high drama emotionalism that can't be shrugged off. You're a strange blend of detachment and overblown passion. You can switch feelings on and off for seemingly no reason. Astro weirding: You cherish the crush.

# Or your Psyche is in...

### ARIES

Ever seen the movie where the main character wants to throw off their sangfroid and just openly pursue the object of their lust? This is your story, Aquarius, when you have Psyche in Aries. You may talk about your freedom and being free from the chains of love, but when your secret love nature is revealed as Aries, you have some changes to implement. Aries is all about rescuing good sorts from dragons. You thrill to the chase, the challenge and/or the opportunity to save someone, whether they like it or not.

### TAURUS

Quiz: Do you shirk your bedwork load by pretending it's not really your thing, but have a niggling desire to be The Natural? When you lot have Psyche in Taurus your secret love nature is that of the über-physical, sensually confident Cow people. The trick to the Psyche is that it has to be worked at — to be unlocked. If you stop fighting it, the Taurean gift of physical pleasure is right there, waiting. Other ways of evoking the gifts of your sensual and fulfilling Psyche sign is to grow flowers, bake cakes, have a massage.

### GEMINI

Sun in Aquarius and Psyche in Gemini! You are a slippery customer! You could live in your head, refusing to condescend to the masses by not feeling anything. As long as things are kept on the intellectual plane, you are one of the most charming people on the planet. But when the tryst moves toward commitment, true love and trust, your Psyche in Gemini baulks. Aqua values honesty but Gemini will say anything to protect privacy and freedom.

## CANCER

Aquarians can take your 'freedom' in a relationship to absurd lengths. Your need not to be tied down lands you virtually on the Moon. However, if your secret love nature is influenced by Psyche in Cancer, there could be a very clingy theme that you are not giving voice to. There is a strong need to be closer to your mate but this is something you'll have to work on. You also have clandestine nurturing, guilting and corrective nagging urges. Compared with the classic Aqua-Maddie you're EQ (Emotional Intelligence) is at genius level.

## LEO

While you are witty, charming and lovable, you are, perhaps, not that openly affectionate. Why? Because of your Psyche in Leo, there is a totally luvvie show pony waiting to get out of that coldish exterior of yours. The Leo influence is your secret romantic self — the person who wants to dance, sing and generally dazzle the person you adore. Yes, you need to discover your inner vain, glorious, performance-artiste diva personality. Any form of creativity is good for you and for your soul!
Vow now: To never think you can do without love.

## VIRGO

Aquarians are known for being great lovers mentally but not really following through on the hurly-burly aspects. But when you have Psyche in Virgo, you have a secret romance identity as a sexual sophisticate and a worldly sensualist with high standards. Aquarians should do what they can to trigger this Psyche aspect of their love life. Why not start by hanging out with people who are more driven physically. They will inspire you. How to deal with your Aqua moods? You could easily cure them via the Virgoan arts of administrivia and wellbeing jags.

## LIBRA

Aquarius is forever looking for the cool people to hang out with and eventually to mate with. Aqua-Maddies are drawn to cool. But when you have Psyche in Libra your love secret is going to be that you are unashamedly drawn to beautiful people. It's not really snobbery — you love the symmetrical features and the balance of the face. You love the fact that these people are gorgeous no matter which angle you view them from. In spite of your own best intellectualizing of your motives, beauty gets you every time. Unfortunately, this goes against your cool act. Sort it! Psyche in Libra is also able to be spiritually enlightened by beautiful fragrance.

## SCORPIO

Secretly wanting more? Keeping the part of you that cares hidden away? The standard Aquarius act of keeping a distance from the ones you love is going to feel more and more strange if you have Psyche in Scorpio. Under this influence, you are forced to admit (if only to yourself) that you would rather be pulling the intensely loyal and mildly jealous act with your loved one. Trying to incorporate this repressed part of your personality into the open part could be challenging as well as fun.

## SAGITTARIUS

Consider it confirmed. Your Aquarian desire to have a trophy lover living at home while you flit off on your adventures with a bunch of cool people is basically supported by your Psyche in Sagittarius. Saggos also like to stay mobile and keep active. There's just one large difference between the two: Psyche in Saggo is the energy of someone who wants spousie along on all the adventures. A nice mix? It's divine.

Astro karma: To hook up with someone who needs your gorm and optimism. They give you emotional sustenance.

## CAPRICORN

Are you a secret materialist? All of the ideological stuff you bang on with is most often about rejecting materialism. However, when you have Psyche in Capricorn you may at some point have to own up to the idea that you not only like financial security, but that you also like your mate to be part of the plan to gain it. Living one side of your life preaching on a soapbox, and the other in the arms of an avaricious lover, is your destiny. Ideally, you combine the two, working within the system to effect real change. On the negative side, you could reject a lot of potentially suitable mates because of the fiscal vibes. Learn to be reasonable.

## AQUARIUS

You are totally comfortable with who and what you are in the love game. Not only do you like to flex your intellectualism and crack a few weird jokes, but your secret love nature as explained by Psyche in Aquarius wants you in that space, too. You are probably destined to find the lover who doesn't mind holding the fort while you go out and have long-winded conversations about eccentric topics. Jilt the jaded lovers who insist on trying to force you into their own so-narrow paradigm. You're an über-original.

## PISCES

Secretly an emotional swamp? With Psyche in Pisces, you lot have a secret love nature that is far removed from the arid love life you like to construct for public consumption. Psyche in Pisces craves a surreal degree of fated love — for example, utter immersion and flashbacks to past lives spent ruling the city of Atlantis together. So, yes, no matter how rational and distant you like to be, you have an inner romantic teenager inside you. Don't try to be too 'mature' about love or relationships. You have the gift of keeping that spark alive indefinitely.

# If you are a Pisces...
## January 21 to February 19

You are the genius flake, the worldly adolescent, the miracle worker who can't drive. In relationships you are plain impossible. In spite of your intellect you swing between a wise knowingness and an infuriating immaturity. You are charming and a great lover. But your OTT tantrums, or your taking dreams seriously, can put too-straight lovers under pressure. Your motto is 'I believe', and this trait – cute at first – can drive people nuts when they realize that you don't just throw the I-Ching for effect, that you do think animals can talk. Most of all, Pisceans know about sex and power: 'You can only sleep your way to the middle'. – actress Sharon Stone.

# and your Eros is in...

# How your Sun sign gets it on with Eros & Psyche

## ARIES

You are Yin and the Ram is Yang. Hey, this could be fun! The mystery of how the Piscean mind works is a matrix-like adventure with no definitive answer. But, if you're looking for a slightly more straightforward love nature, you are in luck: Eros in Aries is like someone taking all of your funny games and manipulations and turning them into an 'on' or 'off' switch. Pisces with Eros here are still complicated and difficult people but they are far less eccentric in a relationship or in the pursuit of love — you don't have the urge to reel someone in just for the fun of it. Eros in Aries is about passion and action and it's very hard to establish your habit of lying. This combo boosts energy, spunkiness and self-belief.

## TAURUS

Getting too cerebral? Pisceans can be a bit sleazy when they are young, but as they mature they run the risk of making their love life a bit too emotional or even metaphysical. Eros in Taurus blasts you out of that by making you highly focused on the natural sensuality that Venus affords. Pisceans can blossom under this love nature because, when love is influenced by Taurus, the physical side of things is so natural that there are no freak-outs — of the type that Fishies are known for. Think Zen — the fish.

## GEMINI

When a Pisces has Eros in Gemini, they have a lot of choices as to the ethical basis for their behaviour. Other Eros signs may keep you on track, but Gemini? It is the one influence that will make you a lot more likely than before to lie, manipulate and use people for your own ends. The best part of Eros in Gemini for you lot is that it creates the impetus to communicate after the first date — one of your pet hates. And, all right, it hypes your cuteness to practically criminal levels. You're charmed and dangerous.

# Soulmating

## CANCER

Whimsical Pisces You goes your own sweet way, whenever you feel like it. Similarly, your Cancerian Eros does whatever it wants, while always justifying it in a huge emotional acting-out orgy, of course. You're compassionate, clever and pre-hysterical a lot of the time. You are almost certainly psychic. In love, you baffle lovers by being doting and over-nurturing or control-freaky one moment and utterly not there the next. You are kind-hearted in the morning but jaded and cynical by midday. People will either hate you or become addicted to your presence.

## LEO

Reconstructing your love nature to make superficial what is already mysterious? Try tapping into your romance persona, Eros in Leo. The Leo influence lifts you out of a fairly tricky personality. It's not really that you are a liar, but you do like to avoid people trapping you emotionally or being put in a position where you have to match what you say with the 'facts'. The Eros in Leo takes you out of that space and more into the gauche show-off. It's not that you don't lie, it's more that you no longer have the time with the costume changes and grooming demands. Frustrated? Then act!

## VIRGO

Pisceans can dwell a little too long in the adolescent space when it comes to pursuing romance. It's not intentional — it's just an easy way to stop certain persons from getting close enough to think they can crush the Fishie specialness. But Eros in Virgo is the love nature energy that could easily give you lot the confidence to be a little more adult and forthright about your relationships. Go with the Virgo feeling and allow yourself to become more of the vampish Virgoan sophisticate.

Your destiny: Ordered love without the tantrums.

## LIBRA

What if you Pisceans had a chance to have a force some along and even out all those ups and downs and shrieking outbursts or sleazy stunts that you get up to when love is around? Would you take it? For those with Eros in Libra, an evening out is exactly what you get. Libra loves to balance out the extremes and find a happy middle — somewhere between the manic stirrer Fish and the neurotic phobic Pisces. In other pursuits of your life, you may not want this 'Stepford' approach, hating as you do any tinkering with your subconscious. But in love? It's a good thing.
Astro flash: You flirt.

## SCORPIO

Pisces with Eros in Scorpio really have to work at staying on an even keel. You're already quite strange and not at all an easy proposition in the relationship stakes. But, here you are with your love nature deeply affected by Scorpio. This means increased intensity and wild paranoid imaginings of conspiracies to commit adultery. It also means intense loyalty and a commitment to stay and work things out — a trait hardly in the standard Piscean love manual. Along with all the depth? You're a seduction diva.

## SAGITTARIUS

With Eros in Sagg, you could be airing out your mind with some much-needed travel. You are not a great traveller in the tourist sense — you much prefer the luxuries of home and you travel only if there's a reason for it. But with Saggo ruling your love nature, relationships go hand in hand with moving about the place. Or, they manifest as love blending with expansion of your mind! You can't for a moment fancy anyone whose principles are not right on.
Astro destiny: There's a stranger in a strange land. Your true love may be a foreigner.

## CAPRICORN

Pisces can be their own worst enemies in the love game — too much following the instincts and reacting to impulses (and dreams) and not enough due diligence about who these people are. But with the powerful influence of Eros in Capricorn you have the outlook that if someone is not signed on to your corporate goals and your performance benchmarks, then the person is a dud. This adds an important aspect to the Piscean personality and can be used to great effect as a filter.

Astro bonus: You get physical self-discipline!

## AQUARIUS

At first glance, Pisces and the Eros-in-Aquarius influence would appear to be quite similar: eccentric, intelligent, hard to pin down. But, look closer and you find that with Eros where it is, you are more likely to be able to put a lover in his/her place. The pure Piscean lover tends to attract people with something to prove whereas the Aquarian energy is about keeping their lover distant enough that they can essentially divide their life into home and life. It's a sense of total control but without the Piscean freakery.

## PISCES

Is anyone up for what you have to offer? You're a Pisces with Eros in Pisces — a love combo that is really not a good idea for so many of those who put themselves forward as The One. You are mysterious, complicated, tempestuous and in touch with worlds that most don't know exist. Your amazing intellect, creativity and bed skills are just the beginning. To follow is your fibbing and the way that any hint of neglect is rewarded with an extramarital fling or the threat of such. The Pisces with Eros in Pisces is the archetypal high-maintenance lover, requiring almost as much understanding as forgiveness. You're demanding, but worth it.

# Or your Psyche is in...

## ARIES

Affairs that start promisingly, then go nowhere, may have something to do with your inability to be direct with your romantic interests. It's a pity because you're sitting on an asset, your Psyche in Aries, which, if you want to work on it, is a perfect way to get rid of some of the passive aggression in your relationships. The next time you feel a petty manipulation coming on, think about the direct and passionate energy that Aries brings. Astro hint: Fitness pursuits help evoke it.

## TAURUS

There is a skittish quality about Pisces who are chasing love. You get funny about the smallest things and start either panicking or lying. A personal challenge – and possibly an aid to you – is the existence in your internal Cosmos of the Psyche-in-Taurus energy. This combo is ruled by Venus and earths you in your body. It's not as deep as it sounds. Taureans are good lovers and totally at home in their bodies. This Psyche aspect is there for your taking. Get it on!

## GEMINI

Have you had an experience where a person you were pursuing suddenly turned into a pumpkin and you've been ducking them ever since? Sounds truly Piscean, right? Well, Geminis are twice as bad at this. However, they do have the saving quality that, rather than hiding from a certain person, they bluff and charm their way out of it. With Psyche in Gemini, you have the ability to tap into this energy and work on your social skills. They do count in soulmating. To consider: Do you live in parallel worlds?

## CANCER

There is something fractured about the Piscean — when it comes to developing relationships they are only ever giving away small snippets of their overall selves. It's fine for brief liaisons, but what about building love with The One? Luckily, you have Psyche in Cancer — your secret love nature and the influence that can draw you into giving more of yourself and creating a nurturing environment along the way. Wouldn't you like to try some caring rather than always being the one who's being cared for?

## LEO

Secretly wanting to put on a show? One of the theatrical things about you Pisceans is the strength of your tantrums. They are quite operatic. However, with Psyche in Leo, you may be covering up a secret desire to play-act and show off, a desire that takes you out of the swampy mysteries of your mind and into a more demonstrative space. Say what you want about Leos — that they are tantrum-throwing show-offs who think they own the limelight — but, they are still able to show their feelings in a free and open manner that doesn't involve intrigues. Tap into this great gift. Go and perform! Expressing creativity is your birthright.

## VIRGO

Pisceans often have slutty stages in their love lives, especially when they're younger and they love the sound of their own charm. However, when you have Psyche in Virgo, your love nature has the potential to be transformed into something more sophisticated and discerning. The Virgo energy is also very worldly in the ways of love. Pisceans are worldly in love, too, but a Psyche in Virgo can pick a person's kink before things get to sex.

Astro flash: Your 'inner Virgo' ensures that you will always be able to perk yourself up via household filth purges and decluttering.

## LIBRA

A secret looks-snob? You Pisceans like to think that you are attracted to people for reasons that are more than just skin deep. And, often you prove this correct. However, with Psyche in Libra your secret love nature is totally into looks as the first and most important filter. By accepting this Psyche, you lot reserve the right to limit your trawlings to the 'drop-dead gorgeous' variety. It's also an energy that helps you balance emotions and aesthetically harmonize your soul so that it's almost as pretty as your face. Do you dither? Yes. Maybe no? But so what?

## SCORPIO

When you're ready to settle on one mate, you'll be glad you have Psyche in Scorpio sitting there as your secret love nature. Scorpio in relationships is the energy that can be a little obsessive but is really just totally intense about the relationship. Even during your flighty and flirty episodes, this could have been a personality trying to break through and be accepted by you. If you're trying to drop the 'date, mate and hate' act from your repertoire, you're in luck with the Scorpio Psyche.

Astro weirding: You're a brilliant interpreter of dreams.

## SAGITTARIUS

You Fishies can get trapped in your safe little places like your bedrooms, your minds or your baths. When they're inside themselves there is a whole ocean for Pisces to explore, but people are so often a drag! Perhaps there's a more expansive way to run a love life? Your Psyche is in Sagittarius — the action traveller of the love-scope who gives gregariousness a good name. It's a secret side of your nature that you are probably repressing, but it could be the real you. To evoke it? Fly off to a great beach. Try an extreme sport. Get involved in politics.

## CAPRICORN

Why do you have such a problem with the so-called straights? Have you ever gone out with one? Well, okay, have you ever given one a second chance? Don't scoff at this — your Psyche is in Capricorn, the Sun sign of people with good jobs, good prospects and stable finances. It's the sign of straights and it's fundamental to your love life when you choose to accept it. That niggling sound is your Psyche telling you that a stable lover with a real job may be a good bet for a change. Or could that person be you?

## AQUARIUS

The Piscean who says 'Yes' to their Psyche in Aquarius is inviting themselves to step up a grade of seriousness. The Piscean motto is 'I believe' while the Aquarians say 'I know'. What Pisceans believe is not often appropriate for public consumption, the things that an Aquarian knows have to be put out there to prove how smart they are. If you can hook into this Psyche of yours, igniting your secret love nature, you get to keep your mystery but communicate on a more accessible level. It may be that Psyche in Aquarius for the Fish is the energy that urges you out of the subjective space and into a realm where a lover has many motivations, the least of them being to irritate you.

## PISCES

It's not a secret any more! With Psyche in Pisces, you really do have an excuse to lead lovers on and then dump them. Also, you are allowed to throw titanic tantrums that bring restaurants to a halt or drop a promising lover because you didn't like the way they spoke to you in a dream. With this Psyche operating in your love nature, you can behave to the utmost of your creative brilliance and still sleep as much as you want. And be loved for it. You just need to find kindred souls and devotees!

'Many waters cannot quench love,
nor can the floods drown it.'

*Song of Solomon* — The Bible

# Ephemeris: Eros

## All dates are inclusive

## 1920

1 January — 6 January in Aquarius
7 January — 15 February in Pisces
16 February — 26 March in Aries
27 March — 5 May in Taurus
6 May — 4 June in Gemini
5 June — 14 July in Cancer
15 July — 13 August in Leo
14 August — 12 September in Virgo
13 September — 22 October in Libra
23 October — 1 December in Scorpio
2 December — 31 December in Sagittarius

## 1921

1 January — 20 January in Sagittarius
21 January — 11 March in Capricorn
12 March — 10 May in Aquarius
11 May — 31 December in Pisces

## 1922

1 January — 5 January in Pisces
6 January — 14 February in Aries
15 February — 26 March in Taurus
27 March — 25 April in Gemini
26 April — 25 May in Cancer
26 May — 24 June in Leo
25 June — 3 August in Virgo
4 August — 12 September in Libra
13 September — 22 October in Scorpio
23 October — 11 December in Sagittarius
12 December — 31 December in Capricorn

# Soulmating

## 1923

1 January – 30 January in Capricorn
31 January – 21 March in Aquarius
22 March — 10 May in Pisces
11 May – 29 June in Aries
30 June — 18 August in Taurus
19 August – 27 September in Gemini
28 September – 27 October in Cancer
28 October – 6 December in Leo
7 December – 31 December in Virgo

## 1924

1 January – 5 January in Virgo
6 January – 24 February in Libra
25 February – 4 April in Scorpio
5 April – 3 July in Libra
4 July – 11 September in Scorpio
12 September – 10 November in Sagittarius
11 November – 30 December in Capricorn
31 December in Aquarius

## 1925

1 January – 18 February in Aquarius
19 February – 9 April in Pisces
10 April – 19 May in Aries
20 May – 28 June in Taurus
29 June – 28 July in Gemini
29 July – 6 September in Cancer
7 September – 6 October in Leo
7 October – 5 November in Virgo
6 November – 15 December in Libra
16 December – 31 December in Scorpio

## 1926

1 January – 24 January in Scorpio
25 January – 5 March in Sagittarius
6 March – 20 November in Capricorn
21 November – 31 December in Aquarius

## 1927

1 January – 9 January in Aquarius
10 January – 29 February in Pisces
1 March – 9 April in Aries
10 April – 19 May in Taurus
20 May – 18 June in Gemini
19 June – 18 July in Cancer
19 July – 27 August in Leo
28 August – 26 September in Virgo
27 September  5 November in Libra
6 November – 15 December in Scorpio
16 December – 31 December in Sagittarius

## 1928

1 January – 24 January in Sagittarius
25 January – 14 March in Capricorn
15 March – 13 May in Aquarius
14 May – 20 September in Pisces
21 September – 19 November in Aquarius
20 November – 31 December in Pisces

## 1929

1 January – 18 January in Pisces
19 January – 27 February in Aries
28 February – 29 March in Taurus

# Soulmating

30 March – 28 April in Gemini
29 April – 7 June in Cancer
8 June – 7 July in Leo
8 July – 16 August in Virgo
17 August – 25 September in Libra
26 September – 4 November in Scorpio
5 November – 24 December in Sagittarius
25 December – 31 December in Capricorn

## 1930

1 January – 12 February in Capricorn
13 February – 3 April in Aquarius
4 April – 23 May in Pisces
24 May – 12 July in Aries
13 July – 31 August in Taurus
1 September – 20 October in Gemini
21 October – 29 November in Cancer
30 November – 31 December in Leo

## 1931

1 January – 8 January in Leo
9 January – 28 May in Virgo
29 May –27 July in Libra
28 July – 25 September in Scorpio
26 September – 14 November in Sagittarius
15 November – 31 December in Capricorn

## 1932

1 January – 3 January in Capricorn
4 January – 22 February in Aquarius
23 February – 12 April in Pisces

13 April – 22 May in Aries
23 May – 1 July in Taurus
2 July – 10 August in Gemini
11 August – 9 September in Cancer
10 September – 9 October in Leo
10 October – 18 November in Virgo
19 November – 18 December in Libra
19 December – 31 December in Scorpio

## 1933

1 January – 27 January in Scorpio
28 January – 18 March in Sagittarius
19 March – 16 July in Capricorn
17 July – 14 September in Sagittarius
15 September – 23 November in Capricorn
24 November – 31 December in Aquarius

## 1934

1 January – 22 January in Aquarius
23 January – 3 March in Pisces
4 March – 12 April in Aries
13 April – 22 May in Taurus
23 May – 21 June in Gemini
22 June – 31 July in Cancer
1 August – 30 August in Leo
31 August – 29 September in Virgo
30 September – 8 November in Libra
9 November – 18 December in Scorpio
19 December – 31 December in Sagittarius

# Soulmating

## 1935

1 January – 27 January in Sagittarius
28 January – 28 March in Capricorn
29 March – 27 May in Aquarius
28 May – 15 August in Pisces
16 August – 3 December in Aquarius
4 December – 31 December in Pisces

## 1936

1 January – 22 January in Pisces
23 January – 2 March in Aries
3 March – 11 April in Taurus
12 April – 11 May in Gemini
12 May – 10 June in Cancer
11 June – 20 July in Leo
21 July – 19 August in Virgo
20 August – 28 September in Libra
29 September – 7 November in Scorpio
8 November –27 December in Sagittarius
28 December – 31 December in Capricorn

## 1937

1 January – 15 February in Capricorn
16 February – 6 April in Aquarius
7 April – 26 May in Pisces
27 May – 25 July in Aries
26 July – 23 September in Taurus
24 September – 31 December in Gemini

## 1938

1 January – 2 March in Gemini
3 March – 1 April in Cancer
2 April – 11 May in Leo
12 May – 20 June in Virgo
21 June – 9 August in Libra
10 August – 28 September in Scorpio
29 September – 17 November in Sagittarius
18 November – 31 December in Capricorn

## 1939

1 January – 6 January in Capricorn
7 January – 25 February in Aquarius
26 February – 16 April in Pisces
17 April – 5 June in Aries
6 June – 15 July in Taurus
16 July – 14 August in Gemini
15 August – 23 September in Cancer
24 September – 23 October in Leo
24 October – 22 November in Virgo
23 November – 31 December in Libra

## 1940

1 January in Libra
2 January – 10 February in Scorpio
11 February – 31 March in Sagittarius
1 April – 9 June in Capricorn
10 June – 7 October in Sagittarius
8 October – 6 December in Capricorn
7 December – 31 December in Aquarius

# Soulmating

## 1941

1 January – 25 January in Aquarius
26 January – 16 March in Pisces
17 March – 25 April in Aries
26 April – 25 May in Taurus
26 May – 4 July in Gemini
5 July – 3 August in Cancer
4 August – 2 September in Leo
3 September – 12 October in Virgo
13 October – 11 November in Libra
12 November – 21 December in Scorpio
22 December – 31 December in Sagittarius

## 1942

1 January – 9 February in Sagittarius
10 February – 31 March in Capricorn
1 April – 16 December in Aquarius
17 December – 31 December in Pisces

## 1943

1 January – 4 February in Pisces
5 February – 16 March in Aries
17 March – 15 April in Taurus
16 April – 15 May in Gemini
16 May – 24 June in Cancer
25 June – 24 July in Leo
25 July – 2 September in Virgo
3 September – 2 October in Libra
3 October – 21 November in Scorpio
22 November – 31 December in Sagittarius

# 1944

1 January – 19 February in Capricorn
20 February – 9 April in Aquarius
10 April – 8 June in Pisces
9 June – 17 August in Aries
18 August – 15 November in Taurus
16 November – 31 December in Aries

# 1945

1 January – 4 January in Aries
5 January – 23 February in Taurus
24 February – 25 March in Gemini
26 March – 24 April in Cancer
25 April – 3 June in Leo
4 June – 3 July in Virgo
4 July –22 August in Libra
23 August – 11 October in Scorpio
12 October – 30 November in Sagittarius
1 December – 31 December in Capricorn

# 1946

1 January – 19 January in Capricorn
20 January – 10 March in Aquarius
11 March – 29 April in Pisces
30 April – 8 June in Aries
9 June – 18 July in Taurus
19 July – 27 August in Gemini
28 August – 26 September in Cancer
27 September – 5 November in Leo
6 November – 5 December in Virgo
6 December –31 December in Libra

## 1947

1 January – 4 January in Libra
5 January – 13 February in Scorpio
14 February – 11 October in Sagittarius
12 October – 10 December in Capricorn
11 December – 31 December in Aquarius

## 1948

1 January – 29 January in Aquarius
30 January – 19 March in Pisces
20 March – 28 April in Aries
29 April – 7 June in Taurus
8 June – 7 July in Gemini
8 July – 16 August in Cancer
17 August – 15 September in Leo
16 September – 15 October in Virgo
16 October – 24 November in Libra
25 November – 31 December in Scorpio

## 1949

1 January – 3 January in Scorpio
4 January – 12 February in Sagittarius
13 February – 13 April in Capricorn
14 April – 31 August in Aquarius
1 September – 10 October in Capricorn
11 October – 19 December in Aquarius
20 December – 31 December in Pisces

## 1950

1 January – 7 February in Pisces
8 February – 19 March in Aries
20 March – 28 April in Taurus
29 April – 28 May in Gemini
29 May – 27 June in Cancer
28 June – 6 August in Leo
7 August – 5 September in Virgo
6 September – 15 October in Libra
16 October – 24 November in Scorpio
25 November – 31 December in Sagittarius

## 1951

1 January – 3 January in Sagittarius
4 January – 22 February in Capricorn
23 February – 23 April in Aquarius
24 April – 22 June in Pisces
23 June – 19 November in Aries
20 November – 29 November in Pisces
30 November – 31 December in Aries

## 1952

1 January – 28 January in Aries
29 January – 8 March in Taurus
9 March – 7 April in Gemini
8 April – 7 May in Cancer
8 May – 16 June in Leo
17 June – 16 July in Virgo
17 July – 25 August in Libra
26 August – 14 October in Scorpio
15 October – 3 December in Sagittarius
4 December – 31 December in Capricorn

# Soulmating

## 1953

1 January – 22 January in Capricorn
23 January – 13 March in Aquarius
14 March – 2 May in Pisces
3 May – 21 June in Aries
22 June – 31 July in Taurus
1 August – 9 September in Gemini
10 September – 9 October in Cancer
10 October – 8 November in Leo
9 November – 8 December in Virgo
9 December – 31 December in Libra

## 1954

1 January – 17 January in Libra
18 January – 26 February in Scorpio
27 February – 17 May in Sagittarius
18 May – 15 August in Scorpio
16 August – 24 October in Sagittarius
25 October – 23 December in Capricorn
24 December – 31 December in Aquarius

## 1955

1 January – 11 February in Aquarius
12 February – 23 March in Pisces
24 March – 2 May in Aries
3 May – 11 June in Taurus
12 June – 21 July in Gemini
22 July – 20 August in Cancer
21 August – 19 September in Leo
20 September – 29 October in Virgo
30 October – 28 November in Libra
29 November – 31 December in Scorpio

## 1956

1 January – 7 January in Scorpio
8 January – 26 February in Sagittarius
27 February – 16 April in Capricorn
17 April – 25 July in Aquarius
26 July – 2 November in Capricorn
3 November – 31 December in Aquarius

## 1957

1 January in Aquarius
2 January – 10 February in Pisces
11 February – 22 March in Aries
23 March – 1 May in Taurus
2 May – 31 May in Gemini
1 June – 10 July in Cancer
11 July – 9 August in Leo
10 August – 8 September in Virgo
9 September – 18 October in Libra
19 October – 27 November in Scorpio
28 November – 31 December in Sagittarius

## 1958

1 January – 16 January in Sagittarius
17 January – 7 March in Capricorn
8 March – 26 April in Aquarius
27 April – 5 July in Pisces
6 July – 13 September in Aries
14 September – 31 December in Pisces

# Soulmating

## 1959

1 January in Pisces
2 January – 10 February in Aries
11 February – 12 March in Taurus
13 March – 21 April in Gemini
22 April – 21 May in Cancer
22 May – 20 June in Leo
21 June – 30 July in Virgo
31 July – 8 September in Libra
9 September – 18 October in Scorpio
19 October – 7 December in Sagittarius
8 December – 31 December in Capricorn

## 1960

1 January – 26 January in Capricorn
27 January – 16 March in Aquarius
17 March – 5 May in Pisces
6 May – 24 June in Aries
25 June – 13 August in Taurus
14 August – 22 September in Gemini
23 September – 22 October in Cancer
23 October – 21 November in Leo
22 November – 21 December in Virgo
22 December – 31 December in Libra

## 1961

1 January – 30 January in Libra
31 January – 7 September in Scorpio
8 September – 27 October in Sagittarius
28 October – 26 December in Capricorn
27 December – 31 December in  Aquarius

## 1962
1 January – 14 February in Aquarius
15 February – 5 April in Pisces
6 April – 15 May in Aries
16 May – 24 June in Taurus
25 June – 24 July in Gemini
25 July – 2 September in Cancer
3 September – 2 October in Leo
3 October – 1 November in Virgo
2 November – 11 December in Libra
12 December – 31 December in Scorpio

## 1963
1 January – 10 January in Scorpio
11 January – 1 March in Sagittarius
2 March – 10 May in Capricorn
11 May – 19 June in Aquarius
20 June – 16 November in Capricorn
17 November – 31 December in Aquarius

## 1964
1 January – 5 January in Aquarius
6 January – 24 February in Pisces
25 February – 4 April in Aries
5 April – 14 May in Taurus
15 May – 13 June in Gemini
14 June – 13 July in Cancer
14 July – 12 August in Leo
13 August – 21 September in Virgo
22 September – 31 October in Libra
1 November – 10 December in Scorpio
11 December – 31 December in Sagittarius

# Soulmating

## 1965
1 January – 19 January in Sagittarius
20 January – 10 March in Capricorn
11 March – 9 May in Aquarius
10 May – 31 December in Pisces

## 1966
1 January – 4 January in Pisces
5 January – 23 February in Aries
24 February – 25 March in Taurus
26 March – 24 April in Gemini
25 April – 3 June in Cancer
4 June – 3 July in Leo
4 July – 12 August in Virgo
13 August – 11 September in Libra
12 September – 31 October in Scorpio
1 November – 20 December in Sagittarius
21 December – 31 December in Capricorn

## 1967
1 January – 8 February in Capricorn
9 February – 30 March in Aquarius
31 March – 19 May in Pisces
20 May – 8 July in Aries
9 July – 27 August in Taurus
28 August – 6 October in Gemini
7 October – 5 November in Cancer
6 November – 15 December in Leo
16 December – 31 December in Virgo

# 1968

1 January – 24 January in Virgo
25 January – 12 July in Libra
13 July – 10 September in Scorpio
11 September – 9 November in Sagittarius
30 December – 31 December in Aquarius

# 1969

1 January – 17 February in Aquarius
18 February – 8 April in Pisces
9 April – 18 May in Aries
19 May – 27 June in Taurus
28 June – 6 August in Gemini
7 August – 5 September in Cancer
6 September – 5 October in Leo
6 October – 14 November in Virgo
15 November – 14 December in Libra
15 December – 31 December in Scorpio

# 1970

1 January – 23 January in Scorpio
24 January – 14 March in Sagittarius
15 March – 19 November in Capricorn
20 November – 31 December in Aquarius

# 1971

1 January – 18 January in Aquarius
19 January – 27 February in Pisces
28 February – 8 April in Aries
9 April – 18 May in Taurus
19 May – 17 June in Gemini

# Soulmating

18 June – 27 July in Cancer
28 July – 26 August in Leo
27 August – 25 September in Virgo
26 September – 4 November in Libra
5 November – 14 December in Scorpio
15 December – 31 December in Sagittarius

## 1972

1 January – 23 January in Sagittarius
24 January –13 March in Capricorn
14 March – 22 May in Aquarius
23 May – 9 September in Pisces
10 September – 28 November in Aquarius
29 November – 31 December in Pisces

## 1973

1 January – 17 January in Pisces
18 January – 26 February in Aries
27 February – 7 April in Taurus
8 April – 7 May in Gemini
8 May – 6 June in Cancer
7 June – 6 July in Leo
7 July – 15 August in Virgo
16 August – 24 September in Libra
25 September – 3 November in Scorpio
4 November – 23 December in Sagittarius
24 December – 31 December in Capricorn

# 1974

1 January – 11 February in Capricorn
12 February – 2 April in Aquarius
3 April – 22 May in Pisces
23 May – 21 July in Aries
22 July – 9 September in Taurus
10 September – 29 October in Gemini
30 October – 31 December in Cancer

# 1975

1 January – 26 February in Cancer
27 February – 27 April in Leo
28 April – 16 June in Virgo
17 June – 5 August in Libra
6 August – 24 September in Scorpio
25 September – 13 November in Sagittarius
14 November – 31 December in Capricorn

# 1976

1 January – 2 January in Capricorn
3 January – 21 February in Aquarius
22 February – 11 April in Pisces
12 April – 31 May in Aries
1 June – 10 July in Taurus
11 July – 9 August in Gemini
10 August – 18 September in Cancer
19 September – 18 October in Leo
19 October – 17 November in Virgo
18 November – 27 December in Libra
28 December – 31 December in Scorpio

# Soulmating

## 1977

1 January – 26 January in Scorpio
27 January – 17 March in Sagittarius
18 March – 5 July in Capricorn
6 July – 23 September in Sagittarius
24 September – 2 December in Capricorn
3 December – 31 December in Aquarius

## 1978

1 January – 21 January in Aquarius
22 January – 12 March in Pisces
13 March – 21 April in Aries
22 April – 21 May in Taurus
22 May – 30 June in Gemini
1 July – 30 July in Cancer
31 July – 29 August in Leo
30 August – 8 October in Virgo
9 October – 7 November in Libra
8 November – 17 December in Scorpio
18 December – 31 December in Sagittarius

## 1979

1 January – 5 February in Sagittarius
6 February – 27 March in Capricorn
28 March – 5 June in Aquarius
6 June – 4 August in Pisces
5 August – 12 December in Aquarius
13 December – 31 December in Pisces

# 1980

1 January – 31 January in Pisces
1 February – 11 March in Aries
12 March – 10 April in Taurus
11 April – 10 May in Gemini
11 May – 19 June in Cancer
20 June – 19 July in Leo
20 July – 18 August in Virgo
19 August – 27 September in Libra
28 September – 16 November in Scorpio
17 November – 26 December in Sagittarius
27 December – 31 December in Capricorn

# 1981

1 January – 14 February in Capricorn
15 February – 5 April in Aquarius
6 April – 4 June in Pisces
5 June – 3 August in Aries
4 August – 31 December in Taurus

# 1982

1 January – 9 February in Taurus
10 February – 11 March in Gemini
12 March – 20 April in Cancer
21 April – 20 May in Leo
21 May – 29 June in Virgo
30 June – 18 August in Libra
19 August – 7 October in Scorpio
8 October – 26 November in Sagittarius
27 November – 31 December in Capricorn

# Soulmating

## 1983

1 January – 15 January in Capricorn
16 January – 6 March in Aquarius
7 March – 25 April in Pisces
26 April – 4 June in Aries
5 June – 14 July in Taurus
15 July – 23 August in Gemini
24 August – 22 September in Cancer
23 September – 22 October in Leo
23 October – 1 December in Virgo
2 December – 31 December in Libra

## 1984

1 January – 9 February in Scorpio
10 February – 9 April in Sagittarius
10 April – 19 May in Capricorn
20 May – 6 October in Sagittarius
7 October – 5 December in Capricorn
6 December – 31 December in Aquarius

## 1985

1 January – 24 January in Aquarius
25 January – 15 March in Pisces
16 March – 24 April in Aries
25 April – 3 June in Taurus
4 June – 3 July in Gemini
4 July – 12 August in Cancer
13 August – 11 September in Leo
12 September – 11 October in Virgo
12 October – 20 November in Libra
21 November – 30 December in Scorpio
31 December in Sagittarius

## 1986

1 January – 8 February in Sagittarius
9 February – 30 March in Capricorn
31 March – 15 December in Aquarius
16 December – 31 December in Pisces

## 1987

1 January – 3 February in Pisces
4 February – 15 March in Aries
16 March – 24 April in Taurus
25 April – 24 May in Gemini
25 May – 23 June in Cancer
24 June – 23 July in Leo
24 July – 1 September in Virgo
2 September – 11 October in Libra
12 October – 20 November in Scorpio
21 November – 30 December in Sagittarius
31 December in Capricorn

## 1988

1 January – 18 February in Capricorn
19 February – 18 April in Aquarius
19 April – 17 June in Pisces
18 June – 5 September in Aries
6 September – 5 October in Taurus
6 October – 31 December in Aries

## 1989

1 January – 23 January in Aries
24 January – 22 February in Taurus
23 February – 3 April in Gemini

4 April – 3 May in Cancer
4 May – 2 June in Leo
3 June – 12 July in Virgo
13 July – 21 August in Libra
22 August – 10 October in Scorpio
11 October – 29 November in Sagittarius
30 November – 31 December in Capricorn

## 1990

1 January – 18 January in Capricorn
19 January – 9 March in Aquarius
10 March – 28 April in Pisces
29 April – 17 June in Aries
18 June – 27 July in Taurus
28 July – 26 August in Gemini
27 August – 5 October in Cancer
6 October – 4 November in Leo
5 November – 4 December in Virgo
5 December – 31 December in Libra

## 1991

1 January – 13 January in Libra
14 January – 22 February in Scorpio
23 February – 22 June in Sagittarius
23 June – 1 August in Scorpio
2 August – 20 October in Sagittarius
21 October – 19 December in Capricorn
20 December – 31 December in Aquarius

## 1992

1 January – 7 February in Aquarius
8 February – 18 March in Pisces
19 March – 27 April in Aries
28 April – 6 June in Taurus
7 June – 16 July in Gemini
17 July – 15 August in Cancer
16 August – 14 September in Leo
15 September – 24 October in Virgo
25 October – 23 November in Libra
24 November – 31 December in Scorpio

## 1993

1 January – 2 January in Scorpio
3 January – 11 February in Sagittarius
12 February – 12 April in Capricorn
13 April – 10 August in Aquarius
11 August – 19 October in Capricorn
20 October – 28 December in Aquarius
29 December – 31 December in Pisces

## 1994

1 January – 6 February in Pisces
7 February – 18 March in Aries
19 March – 27 April in Taurus
28 April – 27 May in Gemini
28 May – 6 July in Cancer
7 July – 5 August in Leo
6 August – 4 September in Virgo
5 September – 14 October in Libra
15 October – 23 November in Scorpio
24 November – 31 December in Sagittarius

# Soulmating

## 1995

1 January – 12 January in Sagittarius
13 January – 3 March in Capricorn
4 March – 22 April in Aquarius
23 April – 1 July in Pisces
2 July – 19 September in Aries
20 September – 19 October in Aries
20 October – 18 December in Pisces
19 December – 31 December in Aries

## 1996

1 January – 6 February in Aries
7 February – 7 March in Taurus
8 March – 16 April in Gemini
17 April – 16 May in Cancer
17 May – 15 June in Leo
16 June – 25 July in Virgo
26 July – 3 September in Libra
4 September – 13 October in Scorpio
14 October – 2 December in Sagittarius
3 December – 31 December in Capricorn

## 1997

1 January – 21 January in Capricorn
22 January – 12 March in Aquarius
13 March – 1 May in Pisces
2 May – 20 June in Aries
21 June – 30 July in Taurus
31 July – 8 September in Gemini
9 September – 18 October in Cancer
19 October – 17 November in Leo
18 November – 17 December in Virgo
18 December – 31 December in Libra

## 1998

1 January – 26 January in Libra
27 January – 17 March in Scorpio
18 March – 26 April in Sagittarius
27 April – 24 August in Scorpio
25 August – 23 October in Sagittarius
24 October – 22 December in Capricorn
23 December – 31 December in Aquarius

## 1999

1 January – 10 February in Aquarius
11 February – 1 April in Pisces
2 April – 11 May in Aries
12 May – 20 June in Taurus
21 June – 20 July in Gemini
21 July – 29 August in Cancer
30 August – 28 September in Leo
29 September – 28 October in Virgo
29 October – 7 December in Libra
8 December – 31 December in Scorpio

## 2000

1 January – 6 January in Scorpio
7 January – 25 February in Sagittarius
26 February – 25 April in Capricorn
26 April – 14 July in Aquarius
15 July – 1 November in Capricorn
2 November – 31 December in Aquarius

# Ephemeris: Psyche

All dates are inclusive

## 1920
1 January — 16 January in Aquarius
17 January — 16 March in Pisces
17 March — 25 May in Aries
26 May — 3 August in Taurus
4 August — 31 December in Gemini

## 1921
1 January — 10 May in Gemini
11 May — 29 July in Cancer
30 July — 27 October in Leo
28 October — 31 December in Virgo

## 1922
1 January — 15 April in Virgo
16 April — 5 May in Leo
6 May — 12 September in Virgo
13 September — 21 November in Libra
22 November — 1 December in Libra
2 December — 31 December in Scorpio

## 1923
1 January — 27 October in Scorpio
28 October — 31 December in Sagittarius

## 1924
1 January — 15 January in Sagittarius
16 January — 4 April in Capricorn
5 April — 11 September in Aquarius
12 September — 1 October in Capricorn
2 October — 31 December in Aquarius

# Soulmating

## 1925
1 January — 9 January in Aquarius
10 January — 20 March in Pisces
21 March — 9 May in Aries
30 May — 7 August in Taurus
8 August — 1 December in Gemini

## 1926
1st January — 14 May in Gemini
15 May — 2 August in Cancer
3 August — 21 October in Leo
22 October — 31 December in Virgo

## 1927
1 January — 9 April in Virgo
10 April — 9 May in Leo
10 May — 6 September in Virgo
7 September — 5 December in Libra
6 December — 31 December in Scorpio

## 1928
1 January — 20 October in Scorpio
21 October — 31 December in Sagittarius

## 1929
1 January — 8 January in Sagittarius
9 January — 8 April in Capricorn
9 April — 5 September in Aquarius
6 September — 5 October in Capricorn
6 October — 31 December in Aquarius

## 1930
1 January – 13 January in Aquarius
14 January – 24 March in Pisces
25 March – 23 May in Aries
24 May – 11 August in Taurus
12 August – 31 December in Gemini

## 1931
1 January – 18 May in Gemini
19 May – 27 July in Cancer
28 July – 25 October in Leo
26 October – 31 December in Virgo

## 1932
1 January – 12 April in Virgo
13 April – 2 May in Leo
3 May – 9 September in Virgo
10 September – 8 December in Libra
9 December – 31 December in Scorpio

## 1933
1 January – 24 October in Scorpio
25 October – 31 December in Sagittarius

## 1934
1 January – 12 January in Sagittarius
13 January – 2 April in Capricorn
3 April – 30 August in Aquarius
31 August – 9 October in Capricorn
10 October – 31 December in Aquarius

# Soulmating

## 1935

1 January – 17 January in Aquarius
18 January – 18 March in Pisces
19 March – 27 May in Aries
28 May – 5 August in Taurus
6 August – 31 December in Gemini

## 1936

1 January – 11 May in Gemini
12 May – 30 July in Cancer
31 July – 18 October in Leo
19 October – 31 December in Virgo

## 1937

1 January – 3 September in Virgo
4 September – 2 December in Libra
3 December – 31 December in Scorpio

## 1938

1 January – 18 October in Scorpio
19 October – 31 December in Sagittarius

## 1939

1 January – 6 January in Sagittarius
7 January – 6 April in Capricorn
7 April– 13 September in Aquarius
14 September – 23 September in Capricorn
24 September – 31 December in Aquarius

# 1940
1 January — 11 January in Aquarius
12 January — 21 March in Pisces
22 March — 20 May in Aries
21 May — 29 July in Taurus
30 July — 31 December in Gemini

# 1941
1 January — 15 May in Gemini
16 May — 24 July in Cancer
25 July — 22 October in Leo
23 October — 31 December in Virgo

# 1942
1 January — 7 September in Virgo
8 September — 6 December in Libra
7 December — 31 December in Scorpio

# 1943
1 January — 22 October in Scorpio
23 October — 31 December in Sagittarius

# 1944
1 January — 10 January in Sagittarius
11 January — 30 March in Capricorn
31 March — 31 December in Aquarius

# Soulmating

## 1945
1 January — 14 January in Aquarius
15 January — 15 March in Pisces
16 March — 24 May in Aries
25 May — 2 August in Taurus
3 August — 31 December in Gemini

## 1946
1 January — 9 May in Gemini
10 May — 28 July in Cancer
29 July — 16 October in Leo
17 October — 31 December in Virgo

## 1947
1 January — 1 September in Virgo
2 September — 10 November in Libra
11 November — 30 November in Libra
1 December — 31 December in Scorpio

## 1948
1 January — 15 October in Scorpio
16 October — 31 December in Sagittarius

## 1949
1 January — 3 January in Sagittarius
4 January — 3 April in Capricorn
4 April — 31 December in Aquarius

## 1950

1 January — 8 January in Aquarius
9 January — 19 March in Pisces
20 March — 18 May in Aries
19 May — 27 July in Taurus
28 July — 31 December in Gemini

## 1951

1 January — 13 May in Gemini
14 May — 1 August in Cancer
2 August — 20 October in Leo
21 October — 31 December in Virgo

## 1952

1 January — 4 September in Virgo
5 September — 3 December in Libra
4 December — 31 December in Scorpio

## 1953

1 January — 19 October in Scorpio
20 October — 31 December in Sagittarius

## 1954

1 January — 7 January in Sagittarius
8 January — 28 March in Capricorn
29 March — 31 December in Aquarius

# Soulmating

## 1955
1 January – 12 January in Aquarius
13 January – 13 March in Pisces
14 March – 22 May in Aries
23 May – 31 July in Taurus
1 August – 31 December in Gemini

## 1956
1 January – 6 May in Gemini
7 May – 25 July in Cancer
26 July – 13 October in Leo
14 October – 31 December in Virgo

## 1957
1 January – 29 August in Virgo
30 August – 27 November in Libra
28 November – 31 December in Scorpio

## 1958
1 January – 23 October in Scorpio
24 October – 31 December in Sagittarius

## 1959
1 January – 11 January in Sagittarius
12 January – 1 April in Capricorn
2 April – 31 December in Aquarius

# 1960

1 January — 6 January in Aquarius
7 January — 16 March in Pisces
17 March — 25 May in Aries
26 May — 3 August in Taurus
4 August — 31 December in Gemini

# 1961

1 January — 10 May in Gemini
11 May — 29 July in Cancer
30 July — 17 October in Leo
18 October — 31 December in Virgo

# 1962

1 January — 2 September in Virgo
3 September — 1 December in Libra
2 December — 31 December in Scorpio

# 1963

1 January — 17 October in Scorpio
18 October — 31 December in Sagittarius

# 1964

1 January — 5 January in Sagittarius
6 January — 4 April in Capricorn
5 April — 31 December in Aquarius

# Soulmating

## 1965
1 January — 9 January in Aquarius
10 January — 20 March in Pisces
21 March — 19 May in Aries
20 May — 28 July in Taurus
29 July — 31 December in Gemini

## 1966
1 January — 4 May in Gemini
5 May — 23 July in Cancer
24 July — 21 October in Leo
22 October — 31 December in Virgo

## 1967
1 January — 6 September in Virgo
7 September — 25 November in Libra
26 November — 31 December in Scorpio

## 1968
1 January — 20 October in Scorpio
21 October — 31 December in Sagittarius

## 1969
1 January — 8 January in Sagittarius
9 January — 29 March in Capricorn
30 March — 31 December in Aquarius

# 1970

1 January — 13 January in Aquarius
14 January — 14 March in Pisces
15 March — 23 May in Aries
24 May — 1 August in Taurus
2 August — 31 December in Gemini

# 1971

1 January — 8 May in Gemini
9 May — 27 July in Cancer
28 July — 15 October in Leo
16 October — 31 December in Virgo

# 1972

1 January — 30 August in Virgo
31 August — 28 November in Libra
29 November — 31 December in Scorpio

# 1973

1 January — 14 October in Scorpio
15 October — 31 December in Sagittarius

# 1974

1 January — 2 January in Sagittarius
3 January — 23 March in Capricorn
24 March — 29 December in Aquarius

# Soulmating

## 1975
1 January — 7 January in Aquarius
8 January — 18 March in Pisces
19 March — 17 May in Aries
18 May — 26 July in Taurus
27 July — 31 December in Gemini

## 1976
1 January — 1 May in Gemini
2 May — 20 July in Cancer
21 July — 18 October in Leo
19 October — 31 December in Virgo

## 1977
1 January — 3 September in Virgo
4 September — 22 November in Libra
23 November — 31 December in Scorpio

## 1978
1 January — 18 October in Scorpio
19 October — 31 December in Sagittarius

## 1979
1 January — 6 January in Sagittarius
7 January — 27 March in Capricorn
28 March — 31 December in Aquarius

# 1980

1 January in Aquarius
2 January – 11 March in Pisces
12 March – 20 May in Aries
21 May – 29 July in Taurus
30 July – 31 December in Gemini

# 1981

1 January – 5 May in Gemini
6 May – 24 July in Cancer
25 July – 12 October in Leo
13 October – 31 December in Virgo

# 1982

1 January – 28 August in Virgo
29 August – 26 November in Libra
27 November – 31 December in Scorpio

# 1983

1 January – 12 October in Scorpio
13 October – 31 December in Sagittarius

# 1984

1 January – 20 March in Capricorn
21 March – 31 December in Aquarius

# Soulmating

## 1985

1 January – 4 January in Aquarius
5 January – 15 March in Pisces
16 March – 14 May in Aries
15 May – 23 July in Taurus
24 July – 31 December in Gemini

## 1986

1 January – 9 May in Gemini
10 May – 28 July in Cancer
29 July – 16 October in Leo
17 October – 31 December in Virgo

## 1987

1 January – 1 September in Virgo
2 September – 30 November in Libra
1 December – 31 December in Scorpio

## 1988

1 January – 15 October in Scorpio
16 October – 31 December in Sagittarius

## 1989

1 January – 3 January in Sagittarius
4 January – 24 March in Capricorn
25 March – 31 December in Aquarius

## 1990

1 January – 8 January in Aquarius
9 January – 9 March in Pisces
10 March – 18 May in Aries

19 May – 27 July in Taurus
28 July – 31 December in Gemini

## 1991
1 January – 3 May in Gemini
4 May – 22 July in Cancer
23 July – 10 October in Leo
11 October – 31 December in Virgo

## 1992
1 January – 25 August in Virgo
26 August – 23 November in Libra
24 November – 31 December in Scorpio

## 1993
1 January – 9 October in Scorpio
10 October – 31 December In Sagittarius

## 1994
1 January – 7 January in Sagittarius
8 January – 28 March in Capricorn
29 March – 31 December in Aquarius

## 1995
1 January – 2 January in Aquarius
3 January – 13 March in Pisces
14 March – 22 May in Aries
23 May – 31 July in Taurus
1 August – 31 December in Gemini

# Soulmating

## 1996

1 January – 6 May in Gemini
7 May – 25 July in Cancer
26 July – 13 October in Leo
14 October – 31 December in Virgo

## 1997

1 January – 29 August in Virgo
30 August – 27 November in Libra
28 November – 31 December in Scorpio

## 1998

1 January – 13 October in Scorpio
14 October – 31 December in Sagittarius

## 1999

1 January in Sagittarius
2 January – 22 March in Capricorn
23 March – 31 December in Aquarius

## 2000

1 January – 6 January in Aquarius
7 January – 16 March in Pisces
17 March – 15 May in Aries
16 March – 24 July in Taurus
25 July – 31 December in Gemini